The Official
2017 ANNUAL

Alison Maloney

BBC
BOOKS

CONTENTS

Claudia Winkleman

After meeting the latest celebrities taking the Strictly Come Dancing challenge, presenter Claudia is brimming with glee. And there's one particular political bigwig who has already swung her vote.

'When the producers sat us down and told us the line-up, Tess and I were totally blown away,' she reveals. 'They are all brilliant, fantastic at what they do and, although it's early days, they all seem to be getting on so well.

'But Ed Balls was the one who made me scream! He was on my wish-list last year, and I really wanted him to come on the show. Then the Strictly miracle workers got on to him and I'm so thrilled he said "yes". He's so funny and incredibly kind and he's going to be amazing.'

The former Labour minister is not the only one giving Claudia the giggles in this year's star-studded cast.

'I am already slightly in love with Tameka,' she jokes. 'She makes me scream with laughter and they're all really funny, in the right way. Melvin makes me laugh out loud and I think Lesley and Anton will be hugely entertaining. The banter between Craig and Judge Rinder is bound to be hilarious. You can never tell where the comedy is going to come from – and it's not always from the obvious people.'

When it comes to her tips for the trophy, Claudia is hedging her bets.

'One thing I will say is that I have never ever been right about who will win!' she admits. 'I genuinely don't know. I think Daisy and Laura both look brilliant. Tameka could be amazing. Ore was really good in the launch show dance, and so was Judge Rinder.

I love Will Young. Then there's Claudia. When you watch her do her proper job, as a gymnast, she has got phenomenal rhythm, she's fit and so perfect at what she does, so I think she'll be good. We'll just have to see.'

Although she is now in her third year of co-presenting the show, Claudia confesses to a few pre-show butterflies.

'It's still terrifying because it's live television and things can go wrong, so I do get nervous,' she says. 'But that's what I have to do. It's just my thing. If I was very relaxed it would be weird for me, so I'll just be scared and Tess will look after me.

'I love Tess and it really helps to have her around because we look after each other, but that's what the whole cast and crew are like. All of them are so supportive.

'At the launch show, Lesley Joseph said, "I can't believe it's like this. It's a proper little family." It's true. Everybody is nice; everybody makes sure the others are OK. It's just a lovely atmosphere.'

The bubbly presenter is sad to be seeing the last of one 'family' member, as Len waltzes off into the sunset at the end of this series.

'It's devastating,' she says. 'I can't even talk about it. He is just the loveliest man. He'll be terribly missed.'

Wanted on the dance floor … Jay and Aliona picked up the trophy after a spectacular final

Jay

Jay McGuiness

Singer Jay McGuiness was ecstatic when he took home the coveted glitter ball trophy last Christmas, and he reveals that his bandmates from The Wanted helped him make up his mind.

'I was in America and I wanted to come home, so when Strictly called, it sounded like fun,' he recalls. 'My family and all the boys were behind me, and probably talked me into it, but it turned out to be the best decision ever.'

While his opening cha-cha with partner Aliona Vilani was far from an 'All Time Low' it failed to impress Craig – who gave him a measly 5 – and shy Jay admits he was out of his comfort zone.

'Coming from a group I'm used to having four other people to deflect the limelight so I was suddenly on my own, and had to speak for myself, and that was hard,' he explains. 'The first live show was shocking because I didn't know what I was doing. It was live, and there was an overload of sequins and happy faces, so I was a bit dazed and confused but it was very exciting.'

Above The singer's week 3 Pulp Fiction jive scored a record 37 and helped squash his nerves

Above Jay's week one dance
had Bruno telling him
'We're Glad You Came.'

By week 3, however, Jay had found his feet and his spectacular Pulp Fiction jive knocked the judges off theirs. Despite a record score of 37, the pop pin-up thinks Latin is not quite his style.

'It's all hips and tans and that's not me,' he laughs. 'I had to dig deep to smile in my flowery Hawaiian shirt, so I think ballroom suited my personality more. I'm not naturally very Latin.'

Even so, the 25-year-old still hasn't settled on his favourite dance.

'It's like choosing a favourite song, it depends on your mood,' he explains. 'A nice slow waltz is more relaxing because there are less steps, but I sometimes like a faster dance, and absolutely loved our Doctor Who Charleston.

'A few weeks after, we met Matt Smith's friend and she said he was a big fan and thought it was brilliant, which made me pretty happy. I got the seal of approval from a real Doctor Who.'

Jay admits to being a little nervous of the Strictly wardrobe but he was pleasantly surprised. 'Sometimes they'd start off tame and add more sequins as the week went on,' he says. 'But they are careful not to put you in anything that will make you unhappy because they want you to enjoy the experience. Some people go crazy and it suits them but I was trying not to go out in a feather boa every week!'

The star from Newark says he and Aliona were shocked to take the title because 'everyone danced so well on the final and I thought we had no chance. But it's a viewers' vote so it was amazing to think that so many people had watched and liked what we were doing, because we enjoyed every minute.'

Jiving Jay went on to win almost every night on tour and picked up a second glitter ball trophy.

'I have one on a bookshelf in my bedroom and the other is in my twin brother's downstairs bathroom,' he reveals. 'Tom is really smart and works for a football club and, even though he's only five minutes older than me, he "big brothers" me a lot. So, every time he goes to the bathroom, I want him to remember that I did Strictly and I absolutely smashed it.'

Below Strictly Champ … The pop singer proved he was a dancer and beat his fellow contestants to the top prize

Darcey Bussell

Darcey Bussell is back for her fifth series on the Strictly Come Dancing panel and this time she is feeling something special in the air.

'We're still getting to know the celebrities and their characters but at the launch show the atmosphere backstage was lovely,' she explains. 'Usually everyone is nervous and not sure what to say to each other but this year it wasn't as tense at all and the atmosphere was really relaxed. Everyone was excited and chatting.

'They put on an amazing group dance and the energy in the room was humming. I've never felt a buzz like that before.'

The dancing queen still gets as excited as the celebs do when a new series launches – and loves to see the contestants being paired with their professional dancers.

'I have a little book with all the celebrities' names and my guesses as to who they will be paired with, so I can see how well I do,' she reveals. 'This year, I got about 20 per cent right!'

What do you make of the class of 2016?
It's a good mix as always, but this year the personalities are very strong. Also, having two Olympians so soon after Rio will have a similar effect to that of 2012, which was incredibly exciting. It puts an edge on everybody else because they suddenly know what hard work is. Athletes really know how to put the hours in.

Who stands out as the top dancers?
Will Young is one to watch. He's quite shy but he's very cool. Judge Rinder surprised me. He was great on the dance floor and is obsessed with dance. He was very happy to be teamed with Oksana because he has been learning Russian, just in case he got a dancer who can speak it, which I think is classic.

Who has some surprises up their sleeve?
Ed Balls is very cheeky and that's going to come out in his dancing, big time. There will definitely be a lot of entertainment there. He has a glint in his eye.

Anybody who seems to be struggling?
Greg Rutherford keeps putting himself down and says he only goes in straight lines, so it might be difficult to make a circle! But he also says he will work really hard, and he's keen to learn. He has a great teacher, in Natalie, and she is incredibly patient.

What did you think of last year's dancers?
It was an interesting series because it all changed at week three when Jay did his amazing jive. He set the bar so early, the others thought 'Hang on, I've got to work a bit harder.' Suddenly the change in those who were putting the hours in became apparent and the people who weren't going to improve became more noticeable so there was a definite gap.

How do you feel about losing Len?
It's sad. He's such a personality and he gives such a lot to the show. I hope we do some ballroom numbers especially in his honour and give him a beautiful send-off. He has given me so much and been so patient, because I ask him millions of questions. We're going to miss all of those wonderful sayings, because he was always so funny.

Take them to THE TOWER

Blackpool Tower Ballroom has been the home of dance for over 100 years. The original ballroom, the Tower Pavilion, first opened its doors when the Tower itself was completed in 1894. Within five years, it had proved so popular that the owners decided to reinvest in a grand overhaul with a bigger ballroom designed by Frank Matcham.

Right This is the 1953 team running the Tower – so you have seamstresses, laundry girls, lift boys, maintenance team, upholsterers, gold leafers. Frank recreated it 60 years later and it looks like a paltry team. Maintenance went from 60 to four now.

The design was influenced by the flamboyant Rococo style of the Louis XV period, with intricate plasterwork, rich upholstery, stunning murals, crystal chandeliers and lashings of gold adding to the grandeur of the high-ceilinged ballroom. 'The gold is pure gold leaf, hand applied,' reveals Tower Ballroom manager Kate Shane. 'Sixty years ago there were six gold leafers on the payroll here and there was about £30,000 worth of gold leaf kept in the safe.' At current prices, that would be the equivalent of around £500,000!

The doors opened on 14 May 1899, and featured the new ballroom, a basement circus, a high-end restaurant and an arcade. There was also a huge aquarium, a free-flight aviary and an animal menagerie housing lions and tigers. On its first day an estimated 70,000 people streamed through the doors.

In the ballroom itself, much of Matcham's design remains unchanged with one major exception: the dance floor. In 1956, a devastating fire broke out when a lit cigarette was discarded on the top balcony.

'The blaze burnt the whole dance floor and went into the restaurant below,' explains Kate. 'So today, the balcony frontage and the plasterwork is original but the dance floor was replaced and the fire-damaged artwork restored, although not exactly as Matcham intended. I'm told that the restorers took some artistic licence and made the ladies on the murals more buxom!'

During the war, the ballroom came into its own and served several useful purposes while staying true to its dancing roots. 'It was used during the day for military drilling and sewing parachutes, so the floor would be covered in silk and seamstresses. At night they'd bring in the band for the dance. There are a lot of families here that are the result of local girls who married foreign soldiers after meeting them at the ballroom.'

Unless there is a special event, the venue is open to the public every day except Christmas Day and an annual closure for maintenance.

'Every January we close for two weeks for essential upkeep,' says Kate. 'We sand back the dance floor, take the polish off and smooth out any dents, then we repolish the whole floor. The chandeliers are lowered, using hand winches, then we restore and repair them, double check the bulbs, do a full service and clean and winch them back up. The murals are painted on to canvas and lifted on the ceiling so we can take them down and restore them. After two weeks our ballroom regulars come in to a freshly polished dance floor, and absolutely love it.'

The ballroom is still a thriving dance mecca, with over 300 regulars coming to waltz, foxtrot and quickstep every week.

'Whatever the weather, they come with their dance shoes in their bags to dance to our live organ music.

'You couldn't guess their ages because they look so young. One of our couples is in their late 70s and look like they're in their early 60s – and they're having a great time.

'It's a wonderful place to work because we get paid to make people smile.'

Ballroom bitz

- The dance floor measures 28.9m (94ft 10in) in length and 23.6m (77ft 5in) in width.
- It is constructed from 30,602 different pieces of oak, mahogany and walnut wood.
- The bounciness is created with 21 sets of leaf springs – the sort used in car suspension – under the surface.
- The ballroom is lit by two large chandeliers and 14 smaller chandeliers, 16 'Angel' lights and 38 trio lights.
- The inscription above the stage reads 'Bid me discourse, I will enchant thine ear', a quote from the Shakespeare poem 'Venus and Adonis'.
- Blackpool Tower is made of steel and cast iron. It stands at 158 metres (519ft) tall and weighs 2,586 tonnes.

The Circus

Down in the depths of the Tower Ballroom, far below the famous dance floor, lies a hidden treasure. The Circus is a purpose-built arena in the round, framed by the four steel legs of the Tower, which are embellished with plasterwork.

Here, the Endresz family have been putting on daily shows for families and schools for 25 years, each time with a watery twist.

'The ring sits on a huge tank of water,' explains Kate. 'At the end of every show it drops three and a half feet and fills with 32,000 gallons of water in two and a half minutes for the water and light finale.' Incredibly, The Circus had performing animals as recently as 1991, and they lived in the building. In 1912, they had 40 performing polar bears, four elephants, and numerous tigers and lions housed in the basement. The polar bears were occasionally let outside in the winter months and the elephants were walked up a ramp and across the road to bathe in the sea. There was also a sea lion pool on the roof and, during performances, the creatures would come down slides into the flooded ring.

When ownership of the building passed to Trust House Forte, in 1991, Sir Bernard Delfont, whose wife was a keen animal welfare supporter, banned animals from the show.

The Mighty Wurlitzer

The Tower Ballroom has two organs that play every day. The Roland organ, played by resident organist Phil Kelsall, is permanently onstage but, on the hour, the Wurlitzer rises out of the stage as the organist plays, to the delight of the crowd.

The Mighty Wurlitzer is famous in its own right, having been built in 1939 to the specification of renowned organist Reginald Dixon, resident from 1930 until he retired in 1970. His popular radio broadcasts on BBC Worldwide, featuring the cheerful bouncy notes that became known as the 'Blackpool Sound', made him a household name and he sold more recordings than Bing Crosby.

The Wurlitzer proved mighty indeed, surviving the 1956 fire, and still played to this day.

Right The inscription 'Bid me discourse, I will enchant thine ear', from Shakespeare's poem 'Venus and Adonis', is carved above the stage

Daisy
Lowe

Whatever Daisy Lowe may lack in dance skills, she will certainly make up for in enthusiasm. The London-born model is positively breathless with excitement and can't wait to start strutting her stuff.

'I'm nervous, excited, overwhelmed, joyful,' she reveals. 'I'm trying really hard to be present in the room. It's all so exciting and everyone we're working with is so wonderful and fun, so we're all having a real laugh and enjoying every minute – even if it is tinged with nerves.'

The 27-year-old catwalk queen loves a boogie but says she has never had any formal training and thinks the formal style of ballroom will be toughest for her.

'I love dancing so much!' she says. 'I wouldn't say I'm skilled but I love "Dropping it Lowe", but I've never done anything like this before so this is a whole new territory for me with ballroom. It's the fact you are holding on to somebody else. When I dance with my friends in clubs it's all on your own, so to be in hold with someone else is a completely different thing.

'I'm really excited about the tango, because it's so beautiful and so hard. Hopefully I will make it far enough to do the tango because that's a bit further down the line. But I'm looking forward to all of it. It's such an exciting thing to throw yourself into.'

Daisy, who was raised in Primrose Hill and spotted by a talent scout at the age of 15, has modelled for top designers including Karl Lagerfeld, Vivienne Westwood and Karen Millen as well as gracing the covers of *Vogue*, *Tatler* and *Elle*. Despite a career in the critical world of catwalk, she is apprehensive about the judges' comments.

'It's not going to be easy listening to their criticism,' she admits. 'I love the show and my grandma is a huge fan of Strictly, never misses an episode. Whenever we sit and watch it together, and listen to what the judges say, we go, "Ouch! But I sort of agree." But it's going to be a completely different experience having that put on me, especially after I've poured my heart and soul into it for an entire week.

'It's probably quite character-building. It's also to help you get better. It's constructive criticism, so that you can work on it and get better next time.'

Aljaž
Skorjanec

*Three years ago, on his
Strictly debut, Aljaž clinched the
glitter-ball trophy with catwalk
queen Abbey Clancy.*

Now he's hoping his latest partner Daisy
Lowe will be another model student.
'All three partners I have had have been
brilliant,' he reveals. 'I've had an amazing time
so far and judging by the first weeks with
Daisy, I'm going to have a great time again.

'She's going to do a fantastic job on
Strictly from what I've seen so far. I think
she has huge talent so we need to make sure
we keep working hard. She could be good at
ballroom because she is tall and elegant but
Latin could be great too because she is not
afraid to wiggle!'

The Slovenian dancer won 19 national
championships in ballroom, Latin and Ten
Dance before going professional and touring
with Burn the Floor. He joined *Strictly Come
Dancing* in 2013 and, since winning with
Abbey, has partnered Alison Hammond and
Helen George. His first love is ballroom but
he believes that can often be tricky for non-
dancers to learn.

'It's always a bit hard at the beginning,
because it takes a little while to get used to
the posture and the footwork. Once they
get that and understand that, it's easy to
learn the steps, so I have spent a lot of time
on the technique and the basics to make
sure Daisy is comfortable with those.

'She had never done any ballroom before
we started training and within a few days she
could do a minute and a half of ballroom and
keep her hold, which is amazing.'

At five foot ten, Daisy is the tallest female
contestant in this year's crop and he believes
that makes them a good match on the dance
floor.

'Height can be good but it depends how
tall your partner is,' he explains. 'In our
case, I think the height will work for us. We
both have long legs so we can move a lot in
ballroom and if she kicks beautifully in Latin,
I really think we're in with a good chance.

Over the last few years ballroom boy Aljaž
has got to know Len Goodman well and he
says he is sad to see his mentor go.

'Len has been a huge part of the show
from the very beginning and he is one of
the reasons the show is so special, so I think
he will be hugely missed,' he says. 'I really
get along with him. I am definitely going to
miss him.

Len Goodman

After 12 years on the show, head judge Len recently announced he would be putting down his seven paddle for the last time.

'All good things come to an end and I want to bow out while I still have my wits about me,' he says. 'But it has been an honour and a privilege to have been a part of what no one knew was going to be such a fantastic show.'

The Strictly legend, who took his chair in the first show in 2004, is proud of how far the series has come.

'The progression is amazing,' he muses. 'When I was a boy Roger Bannister broke the four-minute mile and it was a wonderful achievement. As the years have progressed athletes have got better and better. In 1953,

Sir Edmund Hillary climbed Everest. Now they go up it all the time.

'And so it is with Strictly. The dancing just gets more and more accomplished every year and the show has evolved so much. That's the way of the world.'

What are you going to miss most about Strictly?
I will miss my fellow judges but I know they will do a very good job without me. However woebetide anyone who tries to rename Len's Lens. I'm not going to stand for it!

What do you think about this year's competitors?
There are some great potential dancers there but you can't tell and that's what's fascinating. Trying to analyse it is almost impossible. You don't know what's going to turn up and nerves play a great part in it. Some people can just get out there and do it. Others get nervous.

Who do you think has potential?
I would say Danny Mac, Judge Rinder, Tameka, Will Young and Louise. Danny is young and fit and looks like he might be able to dance, and Judge Rinder has a great personality and is not frightened to talk back

to the judges. Tameka is one of the dark horses. What she lacks in technique she will make up for in personality. Last year a singer won and the year before it was a footballer's wife. Louise is both so she ticks two boxes!

Who has the potential to be funny?
Ed Balls. I don't know what his dancing is going to be like but he's got a great personality. Lesley Joseph has got Anton so we can expect some entertaining routines.

Are you excited about the Olympic athletes?
It's great that we have Greg Rutherford – a gold medal in London and bronze in Rio – and a great gymnast like Claudia. I just hope Claudia and AJ don't start sticking in loads of flip-flops and backflips because I don't like that. I didn't like it with Louis Smith. Just because you can do a thing, doesn't mean you have to!

What was your favourite dance of last year?
As much as I thought Jay's jive was fantastic – and it was – for me the dance of the whole series was Kellie Bright doing the Viennese waltz to 'Oom Pah Pah'. Her show dance was great but Jay won the public affection and he really grew in confidence over the series.

Singer Anastacia appeared in series 13 of Strictly Come Dancing as a musical guest – and she fell instantly in love with the show.

'That was our first date,' she jokes. 'It was one kiss and we're done, we're getting married. I got all excited to meet the stars on the show and I was like a little fan girl. Then somebody approached me backstage and said "I heard you really liked the show" and asked me if I would ever think of doing it, so I said, "Sure!" I didn't think they were actually serious!

'But I'm really thrilled. It's an honour to be on the show and I know people who have been on it, and have told me wonderful things about it.'

Anastacia shot to fame in 2001 when her debut single 'I'm Outta Love' became a worldwide smash and went multi-platinum. She followed it with a string of global hits, including the massive 'Left Outside Alone', and eight albums, selling over 30 million records. But she has been plagued with ill health, in 2013, after battling breast cancer for the second time in a decade, she underwent a double mastectomy. Now she's hoping Strictly can help her overcome one of the legacies of the treatment.

'The radical surgeries have left me with a lot of scars on my back so the costumes are going to be challenging,' she admits. 'I'm open to the possibility of showing them but there's no guarantee because I am so very scared of that. All of us women who have been through this have our own fears and showing the scars is definitely mine. Hopefully, this will give me the courage to show them because I am rooting for the women who suffer from breast cancer.'

The 47-year-old American is known for her huge stage presence and dramatic performances, but she promises viewers will see the 'real Anastacia' on the show.

'I'll be completely less confident,' she says. 'I'm going to show so many sides you've never seen but that's the part I like. No one ever sees me with no make-up or sees the Anastacia when she's not onstage, with all the lighting and props. But that's who will be in a rehearsal, you'll see the real me.'

That doesn't mean she'll drop the drama when it comes to the dance floor, however. 'I'm excited about the characters you can be each week,' she reveals. 'I have to be Anastacia every day of my life so this is exciting. I'm going to have multiple personalities on this show and I can't wait to do the theatrical thing.'

Brendan Cole

As one of only two of the show's original dancers, along with Anton Du Beke, Brendan has racked up 13 series.

He started his Strictly career on a high, picking up the very first glitter-ball trophy with newsreader Natasha Kaplinsky.

Since then, he has been paired with the likes of Sarah Manners, Fiona Phillips, Claire King, Kelly Brook, Jo Wood and Michelle Williams, and has made the final on two more occasions, with Sophie Ellis-Bextor and Lisa Snowdon. Brendan and Lisa came third in series 6 – despite getting two perfect scores in the final – and their cha-cha-cha to 'Tears Dry On Their Own' remains the joint best score for that dance.

Brendan was born in Christchurch, New Zealand, and started dancing at the age of six, following in the footsteps of his brother Scott and sister Vanessa, who won last year's *Dancing with the Stars* in their native country. Brendan moved to the UK at the age of 18 with just £1,000 in his pocket and the dream of making it on the professional dance circuit. While paying his way with stints as a roofer and a builder, Brendan and his then partner Camilla Dallerup became the New Zealand and Asian Open Professional Champions and were semi-finalists at the International, UK Open, British Open and World Championships.

His hard work and talent led him to Strictly and he muses, 'You never know what awaits you around the corner.'

Brendan's speciality is Latin American but he adores the foxtrot.

'The foxtrot is a calm, smooth, sexy dance,' he says. 'It just oozes class.'

Last year, Brendan partnered Kirsty Gallacher but they were knocked out after their week 6 Charleston to Lady Gaga's 'Bad Romance'.

'When we got partnered up together I was very excited and I saw somebody who had no dance experience, and not really any performing experience, turn it around and become quite a performer,' he says. 'I was proud of that last performance and I was proud of Kirsty.'

This year he will be dancing with American singer Anastacia, and she couldn't be happier.

'This man is an honour,' she says. 'He is a gem. He has had so much experience that I just want to be the sponge that sucks it up. I can't wait.'

Brendan added: 'Watch this space.'

RECORD BREAKERS

The trophy isn't the only prize to be had for our wannabe ballroom champs. Even those who don't make it to the final can find their way into the annals of history by smashing a previous record. So roll up for our record-breaking Strictly Hall of Fame.

Series 12 champ CAROLINE FLACK has had the most perfect scores with a whopping FOUR times and her dance partner Pasha Kovalev has chalked up EIGHT since starting in Strictly.

JAY MCGUINESS's jive bagged him a record-breaking score of 37 points out of 40, the highest week 3 score in the history of the competition.

The lowest score ever is still the 8 (1, 1, 3, 3) awarded to QUENTIN WILLSON for his series 2 cha-cha. He was dubbed 'Britain's worst dancer' by Craig Revel Horwood and was out before he got a chance to make amends.

So far, JOHNNY BALL has been the oldest competitor ever to hit the Strictly dance floor. He was 71 when he appeared in 2012.

CHELSEE HEALEY is the only celebrity to bag a 40 for the dramatic paso doble, with Pasha, in series 9.

There are only two dances that have yet to yield a perfect score – the rumba and the samba. While four couples have come close in the former, with 39 points, only two (ABBEY CLANCY and Aljaž Skorjanec, FRANKIE BRIDGE and Kevin Clifton) have matched that score in the samba. JILL HALFPENNY, with her partner Darren Bennett, was the first celebrity to score a perfect 40/40, with their unforgettable jive in series 2. It's still the only top-scoring jive.

Series 11 finalist NATALIE GUMEDE has the highest average points across all series, with 36.9. ALESHA DIXON is second with 36.5.

The lowly '1' paddle has only been seen nine times over all 13 series. Unsurprisingly, Craig's was the most frequently dusted off, accounting for EIGHT of them.

Despite coming second in the final, series 7 couple RICKY WHITTLE and Natalie Lowe scored the most 10s in one season, with 28.

The voice of STRICTLY

While he's never seen on screen, Alan Dedicoat, the man with the velvet voice, is as much a part of Strictly Come Dancing *as fake tan and sparkly shoes.*

With tones as smooth as the silkiest ballgown, Alan Dedicoat ushers the celebrities down the iconic staircase at the start of each show, and eases them on to the floor for every dance.

'The show is so popular, that I feel extremely lucky to be associated with it,' says Alan. 'They needed someone to introduce the dancers, the dances and the judges, to help people with who's who, and I fitted the bill. Now, when I meet people, I only have to say "The judges have their scores. Craig Revel Horwood …" and my identity is instantly revealed. It's become my calling card.'

When Alan first lent his dulcet tones to the live show, he was already the working on the BBC lottery show, filmed next door to the Strictly studio at TV Centre. But now that the National Lottery has moved to Pinewood and Strictly has waltzed off to Elstree, he can no longer pop from one to the other so things have to be done slightly differently.

'I pre-record most of my voice overs but we can do last-minute recordings on the Saturday morning, so I do still appear at Elstree,' says Alan. 'The atmosphere is always electric, and I see the excitement and the anticipation of a magical night, which is great. Then I move round the M25 to do the lottery, because that has to be announced live.'

Alan started his career in radio, joining Radio Birmingham at Pebble Mill in 1979 and moving on to local radio in Devon before joining Radio 2 as a newsreader in 1987. Chosen as the 'Voice of the Balls' when the lottery first launched, he took on Strictly in its first series in 2004, and then *Dancing with the Stars* in the US.

'When they were setting up the American show, they asked if they could have the "British guy" to do the announcements,' he laughs. 'So you can't even escape me in America.'

The veteran voiceover man reveals he alters his tone for the various elements of the live show.

'I have to do a massive "shout", which can almost take the lining off your throat.'

'I have to do a massive "shout" as the celebrities come down the stairs, which can almost take the lining off your throat, because you want to grab people right at the start and remind them who is still in the competition,' he says. 'Then I have a softer, more delicate delivery for the "Dancing the paso doble, would A and B please take to the floor…" That's because we've just seen their training video, so you don't need to shout because you are often speaking into a quiet, still studio.

'Then we do specials, like on Halloween night, which gives me a chance to do some silly lines and put on the mock evil laugh, which is great fun.'

Although you'll be hearing plenty of Alan in future series, you won't be catching sight of him on the dance floor.

'I don't think I could dance on Strictly – I've got this bone in my leg,' he jokes. 'I'm not used to hard work!'

Claudia Fragapane

At 18, Claudia Fragapane is one of the youngest contestants to grace the Strictly dance floor.

Despite her tender age, she's at the top of her game when it comes to gymnastics. At the 2014 Commonwealth Games, at just 16, she became the first woman in 84 years to win four golds and, at this year's Rio Olympics, she competed in the team event, coming fifth.

But, while her gymnastic routines require grace, suppleness and musicality, she admits that learning numerous dance numbers will be a challenge.

'My sport will give me a little bit of an advantage but, with gymnastics, I learn one floor routine and stick to that for two years,' she says. 'So I think I will struggle with having a week to learn a dance, and then have another dance the following week. Plus I'm dancing in heels so I feel like I might fall all over the place.'

Although she is in peak physical shape, having trained for the Olympics, Claudia reveals the dance rehearsals initially tested her stamina.

'Being sporty really does help but the dances get your heart pounding and you're still out of breath,' she said. 'My performances are usually 90 seconds, like the Strictly routines, and anything over that and I'm huffing and puffing. But my stint on the show will help with increasing my stamina and teach me different techniques, which I am going to put into my routines when I go back to gymnastics.'

The pocket rocket – who stands at just four foot six – thinks Latin may be her forte because, she laughs, 'I'm not very elegant.

'When I'm training my coach is always shouting "Head up, look taller." I can't look tall – I'm so small. So I think the ballroom will help with the gymnastics by helping me look taller and more elegant. I'm very clumpy and tend to chuck myself around a bit but ballroom will be the opposite of that.'

The Olympic gymnast follows in the footsteps of teammate Louis Smith, who became Strictly champ in 2012.

'I haven't spoken to Louis about the show but once I get a chance I'll talk to him about it and tell him I'm freaking out. I used to watch Louis when he was on the show and saw how he used his gymnastics skills to complement his routines, so I'll be following his lead there.'

The Bristol-born athlete has spent most of her life in leotards so she is happy to don the Latin gear for her dances.

'I'm really looking forward to the costumes, hair and make-up,' she says. 'I love sparkles!'

AJ Pritchard

When the first Strictly Come Dancing aired, AJ Pritchard was just nine years old – and he hadn't even started dancing yet.

Although his dad, who is also a professional, ran a ballroom school, the young AJ was more interested in dancing with danger. 'At the beginning my dad didn't want me to dance because he knew how much hard work it would be, so I only started at the age of 12,' he explains. 'Before that I was snowboarding, quad-biking – anything fast and dangerous! I broke my arm a couple of times. It's all good now but it is a reminder not to show off.'

Born in Stoke-on-Trent, the Strictly new boy made up for lost time after being paired with Chloe Hewitt. Over the last nine years they have been National Youth Latin Champions for a record-breaking three years in a row, from 2012–2014, and in 2015, they won one of the biggest championships in the world to become British Open Youth Latin Champions and European Youth Latin Champions.

Having grown up with the series, the 21-year-old is thrilled to be part of the current Strictly team – and his parents are over the moon.

'It's amazing to be joining the show,' he says. 'My mum and dad were absolutely ecstatic. They think the show is amazing for the dancing world because it's helped highlight what's out there and how good dancing can be for people.'

AJ is dancing with Olympic gymnast Claudia Fragapane, and says her sports background comes in handy in training.

'I'm really happy to be partnering Claudia because she is very hard-working,' he says. 'She has the same mentality as me in wanting to train hard so we're working together fantastically.

'She's finding it hard getting the choreography in order, and trying to remember it all because it's all new to her but she's coming along really well.'

While Claudia follows in the footsteps of Rio teammate Louis Smith, who lifted the glitter ball in 2012, AJ hasn't got his eye on the prize just yet.

'At the moment I'm just concentrating on improving from week to week, trying to get that number down and I'm not really thinking that far ahead. I just want us to be the best we can be each week and see how far it goes.'

But the pocket rockets are planning to give it plenty of zoom when they hit the dance floor.

'Obviously I want to use her gymnastic ability 100 per cent and see what she can do but also what she can teach me, because it's always good to learn.

'Will there be back flips and cartwheels? You never know. You'll have to keep watching!'

Strictly
RITUALS

Saturday is a busy day for the professionals, and each dancer has their own routine to prepare for the live show. Here Aljaž Skorjanec and Karen Clifton take us through their Strictly Saturday.

Aljaž

Saturday is an early start and there's plenty to fit in.

The first thing I do is say 'Hi' to everyone at the Elstree studio – and I mean everyone – because I like them all to start the day with a smile. Then it's straight to wardrobe for a fitting with my celebrity. I make sure I tell them how beautiful they look, because they always do.

After the group dance rehearsal, which is fun, we run through the couple's dance.

If it's a ballroom dance, I check that my tail suit and my shoes look perfect. If it's Latin – which means an open shirt or even no shirt at all – I try to do all the push-ups and sit-ups in the world! A couple of years ago, Anton and I started doing a few every time we saw each other and all the pro boys now join in. It's far too late by this stage to make any difference but it feels better in my head!

As I walk round the studio, I am constantly singing the song we're dancing to that week. It can be pretty annoying but that's how I deal with my excitement.

I don't like to eat too much before a show in case it makes me feel bloated. Instead, I usually snack on some nuts and drink coffee – a lot of coffee – to keep my energy up.

Before we go on I go through the dance with my celebrity, making sure that they are comfortable and giving them a confidence boost.

As we wait in the wings, I always say the same thing: 'It's time to shine.' Then we hit the dance floor.

Karen

It's Saturday. 7 a.m. My alarm goes off and there's only one thing on my mind... It's Strictly time!

I grab a cup of coffee, put my dancing gear on and get in the car for a fabulous day full of glitter, sparkles, feathers and shimmering superstars!

At Elstree, I check my schedule for the day and find my celebrity, then it's straight into hair and make-up to find out what my look is going to be. I spend about 40 minutes in there and snack on bananas to keep me going. Then there's a band rehearsal with my celeb and I cross my fingers that nothing goes wrong – that he doesn't step on my foot or wink at the camera and forget his steps!

Next stop is wardrobe to see my costume, they always make us the most gorgeous dresses. We are very lucky.

At dinnertime, everybody is feeling anxious, excited, a bit nervous but ready to roll. I grab my food and go into the dressing room where all the female pros are. We chat and giggle and, of course, share lots of chocolate.

At last it's show time! We all wait backstage. Some people are stretching or practising their steps. Others are just chatting and joking. The vibes are good.

I go into a corner and take five minutes to get my thoughts together and focus then I do 52 jumping jacks to get my blood flowing. It's always 52 because $5 + 2 = 7$ and 7 is my lucky number. I even have it tattooed on my wrist.

As we wait, I tell my celeb to enjoy every second but not so much that he forgets his steps. Then we hear the magic words: 'It's time to meet the stars of the show.'

We all look at each other, smile and hope. For the best performance ever…

Tess Daly

As ballroom queen Tess Daly digs out the glad rags for her 14th Strictly Come Dancing, she is looking forward to another sparkling series. In fact, the new recruits have already made an impression on her.

'The energy in the room at the launch show was something. 'They were all so excited to be taking part. A few of them told me they'd grown up watching *Strictly* so there's a great affection for the show among the contestants and they now know what to expect. They were all delighted to be there and full of energy and enthusiasm. There was a real frisson in the air and everybody was a bit giddy.'

Tess admits it's hard to put her finger on the likely finalists – but she has been busy talent-spotting.

'Daisy Lowe has a lovely sense of rhythm and she loves to dance. Laura Whitmore looks like a natural dancer. Danny Mac was looking pretty accomplished very early on,

and he'll be popular with the ladies. And Melvin has got some great moves. We all fell in love with him on the show.'

But the savvy presenter also reckons one or two of the contestants will have some surprises up their sleeves.

'Lesley Joseph is incredibly fit with bags of energy,' she reveals. 'She was flying across the dance floor like somebody half her age. The young 'uns will struggle to keep up with her – and so will Anton!

'We watched the group dance rehearsals, where the celebrities meet the pro dancers for the first time, and Ed Balls was a huge surprise because he looks like he can dance. Who'd have thought we'd have the former shadow chancellor doing a cha-cha?'

Whatever the dance skills of the class of 2016, there is plenty of personality, says Tess.

'Tameka and Anastacia are the fun in the room,' she says. 'You know when they've arrived.

'It's also wonderful having two Olympians fresh from Rio and I'm looking forward to seeing what they bring to the floor. Gymnast

Claudia has the potential to wow us, just like Louis Smith. So I'm hoping she'll break out the back flips.

'Greg Rutherford is at the top of his own game but he is way out of his comfort zone because he is used to winning, and being good at what he does, and he says he will be frustrated if he can't get the steps. But he's looking forward to the spray tans!'

Tess admits the final will be more emotional than ever as we say goodbye to Strictly stalwart Len Goodman.

'I am in denial,' she says. 'It's hard to imagine Strictly without him as he's been there since day one. He's a huge part of the show and we'll miss him. But we've been lucky to have him for as long as we have. He is a legend. I will shed a little tear on his last show, without a doubt.'

Danny Mac

As an actor, Danny Mac is used to being in character so he'll have no trouble taking on different personas for each dance. But the former Hollyoaks star is more worried about how he'll come across when he's just being himself.

'I am terrified because the idea of being me on television scares the hell out of me,' he admits. 'I am happy hiding behind scripts and words that are given to me. But I thought it was time to embrace it because, if I don't do it now, I may not get the chance again.

'I would never have done Strictly while I was in *Hollyoaks* because the schedule is too tough but I'm at a point in my life where I am ready for a new challenge and I have the time. The fact that it scares me is a good reason to do it so I thought I'd take it, go for it and completely embrace it.'

The 28-year-old, who quit *Hollyoaks* in 2015 after five years playing Dodger Savage, follows in the footsteps of former cast members Ricky Whittle and Ashley Taylor-Dawson in taking the Strictly challenge.

'Ashley did it while he was still on the show and he had a pregnant fiancée who had the baby during the run,' marvels Danny. 'But

he told me, "You are going to have a brilliant time. Soak it all up. Take all the rehearsal time you can get because it will be the best time of your life." He couldn't even give his entire time to it and he still had a blast, so I had to do it.'

The Bromley-born actor has some dance experience, having starred in the West End musical *Wicked*, and he is hoping that his many young fans will help him get through the first weeks. But he is well aware his feet need to do the talking when it comes to the judges' scores and the public vote.

'It's always going to be down to what you do on the dance floor rather than who you are,' he reflects. 'There are going to be fans of other contestants who won't know who I am because across the board there is such a cross-section of people from so many different places, all wanting to do the one thing we've never done.

'But I really want to learn how to dance and I'm here to do that, so hopefully the judges and viewers will see that. I'm going to take every single bit of the judge's criticism on board because if you are lucky enough to stay that's what will make you better. They're the ones to tell you because they know. I'm nervous but everything they say is going to be spot on.'

Oti Mabuse

Despite an early knock-out with boxer Anthony Ogogo, in her first Strictly outing, Oti is raring to get back in the ring with ex-Hollyoaks actor Danny Mac.

'I am really excited to be dancing with Danny,' she says. 'I could see from the beginning that his heart was in the right place and that's what is important to me. He's working hard, he's enjoying it and having lots of fun. I am still trying to find out what he's good at, what he loves to do, what his body does naturally and because he's giving it 100 per cent it's easier and so far I'm impressed. Everything is going smoothly because he wants it as badly as I do.'

Oti was born in South Africa and began dancing as a child alongside her sister Motsi, who is also a professional dancer. After studying civil engineering at university, she moved to Germany, where she competed on *Dancing with the Stars* before joining the UK show last year. Unfortunately, a shoulder injury sustained by dance partner Anthony in the ring before he started training for the show hampered their progress, and the pair were out in the third week.

'We thought Anthony's injury was going to get better but we found out that he had injured a nerve which was hindering his recovery,' she reveals. 'He gave 150 per cent the whole time but because of his arm, he couldn't really do as much as he wanted in a competition where every movement counts.'

Oti is philosophical about the early exit. 'Last year was a lot of fun,' she says. 'Going out early was actually good for me because I could stand back and watch how other people choreograph, how they teach and create, and it has helped me. I come from a very technical world where all the focus is on the smallest detail but in Strictly it's also about affecting people by entertaining them or touching their hearts and making them feel an emotion. I learnt so much and this year I will be able to bring some of that to my routines with Danny.'

But the soap star will have to be on his toes if he wants to impress his tutor.

'He is very determined so I need to give him the information and the focus and everything else will follow. But I am going to be myself. I am going to be a perfectionist, driven and wanting to see him do the best that he can.

Bling up your BALLROOM SHOES

Good dancers have twinkle toes and, when it comes to Strictly, they twinkle more than most. Before the show, the costume department spend hours hand-gluing hundreds of crystals to create a unique design and make fancy footwork sparkle.

So do you fancy stepping out in the most dazzling dance shoes on the floor? Follow our simple guide to turn your footwear from 'dull, dull, dull' to 'fab-u-lous'.

Choosing your shoes

You can bling up most shoes and even add stones to the heels for that extra wow factor, but if you are intending to go Latin or ballroom dancing, you must make sure you pick the right footwear.

'A dance shoe is very different from a typical shoe,' explains Justin Patel of International Dance Shoes. 'For a competitor on Strictly, as with any dancer, there is a greater requirement for flexibility, and while the shoe has to also be extremely lightweight it also needs to be very supportive, comfortable, balanced and, of course, elegant.

'The sole material is also different, with a suede sole enabling the dancer to gracefully move across the floor.' There are also major differences between the Latin and ballroom style.

'For Latin, ladies' shoes are a sandal design, with the front mainly made up of straps and either a T-bar or wrap-around strap. For both ladies and gentlemen, they'll typically have a higher heel, with many of the girls opting for a slightly skinnier heel.

You can bling up most shoes and add stones to the heels for that extra wow factor.

'For ballroom, the ladies will wear a court shoe with or without a strap. The heel might be a bit lower on the ballroom shoes and generally the men's ballroom shoe will have a 1-inch heel as opposed to the 1.5-inch heel for Latin.'

Getting that Strictly sparkle

Over the years the costume team, led by designer Vicky Gill, has created hundreds of showstoppers with strategically placed crystals. Vicky advises that you think carefully about the placing of the stones.

'When applying crystal embellishment to shoes for dance purposes you have to be very careful on the position,' she says. 'I would recommend that you concentrate the embellishment on the outside area of the shoe. Ballroom and Latin choreography requires the dancer to pass their feet through the centre, so if there is a lot of stoning on the inside of the shoe, you could catch your ankle and that really hurts.

'However, if bling is king for you and your approach is no pain no gain, and it's all about the sparkle, then go for it and cover the whole shoe. Just don't say I didn't warn you!'

'I recently commissioned a shoe that is completely covered in silver embellishment for Joanne Clifton's West End role as Marilyn Monroe and they looked amazing.'

The Strictly team use both crystals and rhinestones though the latter tend to work out a little cheaper.

To start, you will need crystals or rhinestones, and strong fabric glue. 'Most stones are applied to satin material so for this it is important to have a glue that is a permanent adhesive that dries crystal clear and suitable for fabrics,' says Justin.

The Strictly team use both crystals and rhinestones though the latter tend to work out a little cheaper. The various stones, as well as the glue, can be found online and at good craft shops. Vicky also suggests a tub of beeswax to help apply the crystals.

How to Create Your Own Sparkling Strictly Showstopping Shoes

Step by step

- Wipe over the shoe to make sure you remove any dust particles.
- Draw the shape you would like to follow with tailor's chalk if you are not following detailed stitch lines or existing shapes on the shoe.
- Decide on the sizes of crystals that you would like to use. If you are covering a larger area mixed sizes make it easier to fill the shape.
- Place stones in a small container with a flat bottom (a jam jar lid is perfect).

- Apply glue to the chalked area, only covering a small section at a time so that the glue doesn't dry too quickly.

- Place a small amount of beeswax on the tip of a pencil. This makes it easier to pick up the stones.
- Carefully pick up each stone with the tip of the pencil with beeswax on and place on to the glue on the shoe.

- Leave the glue to dry for approximately 6–10 minutes to ensure that everything is set properly.

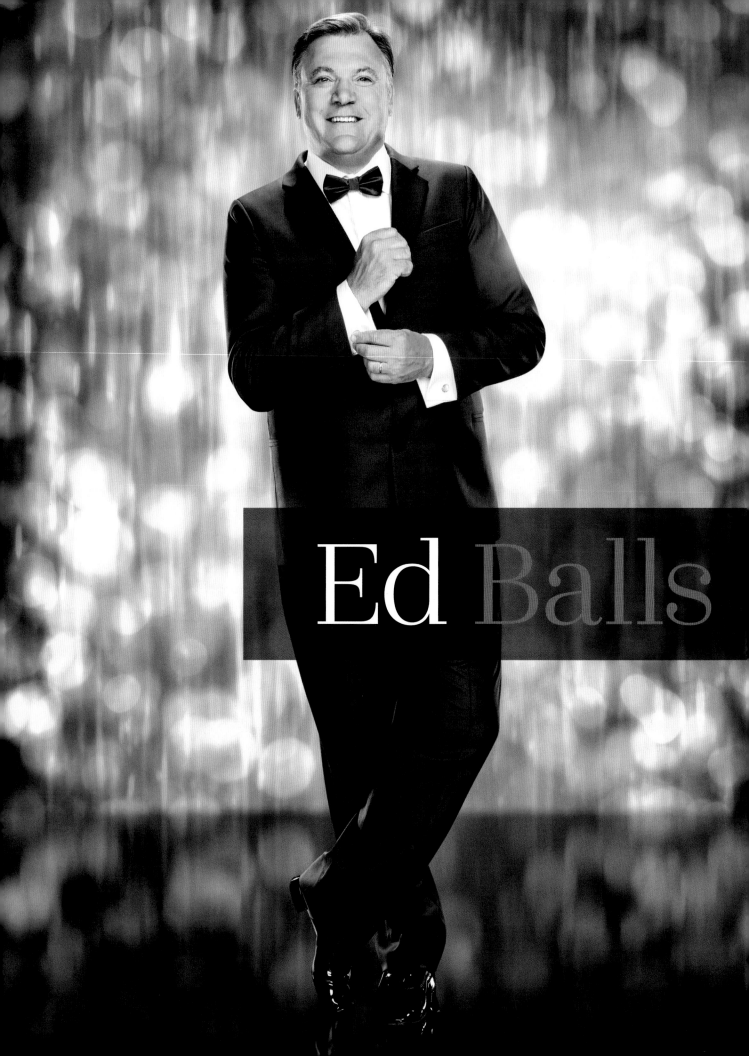

Ed Balls

As a former politician, Ed Balls knows a thing or two about swing, but will his party moves score high in the opinion polls when he takes to the floor?

'I'm quite good at line-dancing, but unfortunately that's not in the show,' he jokes. 'I can waltz, but at the moment I'm struggling with the idea of Latin because apparently it's important to isolate your hips and shoulders. When I try to move either of them, other things move too so I'm quite challenged by the Latin.'

The former shadow chancellor, who lost his seat in the 2015 election, says wife and fellow Labour MP Yvette Cooper was behind his decision to try on the dancing shoes. 'I had a post-politics bucket list,' he reveals. 'I wanted to get more involved with Norwich City Football Club and I really wanted to do Strictly, if they asked me. Even so, I was nervous about it because I'm not sure I'm Strictly material. But Yvette said "you've got to do it" and she's been the biggest push behind me.

'Yvette would love to do it herself. She's deeply envious and she keeps dancing round the house so I'm doing it on her behalf.'

The 49-year-old is determined to give it his all but he admits that, although he is fit, the initial training has been tough.

'I did the marathon three times and I found the first week of dance training, when we did ten till six, as hard as doing the marathon! It was a really intense eight hours.'

Before taking his first steps on the dance floor, Ed talked to former contestant Jeremy Vine, who had some sound advice.

'Jeremy said it was the best thing he's ever done in his life and I should do it like a shot. He also said "You've just got to do as many hours as you can, listen to your professional and just learn."

'I've also had advice through the media from Ann Widdecombe and Edwina Currie and I'm obviously taking on board their helpful tips and hoping to build on their achievements. But I don't think I'll be flying in like Ann did.'

Although he is embracing the cha-cha and looking forward to the Charleston, staunch Labour man Ed thinks he may be a bit conservative when it comes to the outfits.

'I'm not a sequins and glitter type of person so I'm keeping it classic,' he laughs. 'There are people who love to sparkle but I prefer to be a bit careful. I have a problem in that I have three kids and they have very strong views! A lot of things have been vetoed.'

Katya Jones

'The first launch show, with the red carpet, was absolutely incredible,' she says. 'I kept thinking "I am going to remember this night for the rest of my life." Everything from sitting in make-up and hair and getting fitted in costume was amazing, and the reaction of the public was lovely, with people telling me "We can't wait to see you on the dance floor."

'It's not something we're used to because in the competitive world we are judged and officiated but not well known or loved for what we do. It was really nice.'

The Russian dancer was born in St Petersburg and started dancing at the age of six. In 2008 she met fellow Strictly dancer Neil Jones in Blackpool, where he was competing in the British Open, and a few days later they formed a partnership that soon blossomed into romance. The couple, who tied the knot three years ago, are triple winners of the World Amateur Latin Championships and, in 2015, were crowned World Professional Latin Show Dance Champions.

Katya will debut on the dance floor with former shadow chancellor Ed Balls and he is certainly getting her vote so far.

'I am so happy to be dancing with Ed,' she says. 'Especially now I know what kind of person he is. He's the kindest person I've ever met, so down to earth and humble. People know him as a politician, and quite serious, but this gives him a chance to show his human side. He is a normal person who has never done anything like this and he is trying really hard, and working hard, and he's very funny, so I'm grateful I get the chance to show him off as a lovely guy who is giving it a go.

Katya believes he has more potential than some might give him credit for.

'He's doing fantastically,' she insists. 'He's got rhythm and he's musical, because he plays the piano, which is helpful. He hasn't got two left feet at all.

'We are trying to learn a lot of things at the same time and it's not easy. He is physically fit, so stamina is not a problem, but it is mentally challenging more than physically. He's coping really well and picking up steps really quickly.

'I might not tell him a lot, because I want to keep pushing him, but I am quite proud of him at the moment!'

Which JUDGE are YOU?

Are you as bombastic as Bruno, or as classy as Darcey? Find out which of the Fearsome Foursome is closest to you with our fun game.

1 A fan sends you a tin of assorted biscuits. Which one do you choose?

a) Pink wafer – colourful and tasty

b) Lemon biscuit – slightly sour with a kick

c) Digestive – no frill, no nonsense

d) Ladyfinger – elegant and slightly sweet

2 During a break in filming you head off to the green room. Do you?

a) Watch *101 Dalmatians* because you just LOVE Cruella de Vil

b) Tuck into some pickled walnuts

c) Brew up some herbal tea

d) Take the opportunity for a good natter

3 You're choosing where to have a slap-up meal. Which type of restaurant would you pick?
a) Pie and mash
b) Thai
c) Italian
d) High-end French cuisine

4 The waiter drops a tray of glasses. Do you say…
a) That's a drinks disaster, darling.
b) You made mincemeat out of that, what a mess!
c) You need to work on your arm position.
d) You came out here, gave it your all, but that slip will cost you.

5 Settling down for the evening with a good film, but which do you choose?
a) A musical
b) A classic Western
c) A romantic comedy
d) A horror

6 What's your idea of a perfect night?
a) A huge party – the wilder the better
b) A dinner party with lots of friends
c) A quiet meal for two and a cup of tea
d) A slap-up family meal

7 What's your favourite dance?
a) Paso doble – bold and dramatic
b) Samba – party time
c) Rumba – romantic and fluid
d) Foxtrot – Traditional and elegant

Points

1.	a) 2	b) 3	c) 4	d) 1
2.	a) 3	b) 4	c) 1	d) 2
3.	a) 4	b) 3	c) 2	d) 1
4.	a) 3	b) 2	c) 1	d) 4
5.	a) 1	b) 4	c) 2	d) 3
6.	a) 2	b) 3	c) 1	d) 4
7.	a) 3	b) 2	c) 1	d) 4

How Did You Score?

7–11 points: Classy Darcey

You are the epitome of taste and refinement, beautifully composed at all times. Underneath that elegant exterior beats a heart of gold, and you're quick to lend support and advice whenever needed.

12–17 points: Bruno-licious

Flamboyant and fantastic, you are the heart and soul of the party and there's never a dull moment when you're around. Boring isn't an option.

18–23 points: Craig-tastic

You're quick-witted and funny, with a healthy dose of cynicism. You know what you like, and what you don't. You may not suffer fools gladly but you're a loyal and entertaining friend to be around.

24+ points: You're top dog Len

You have a straight-talking, no-nonsense approach to life, tinged with a great sense of humour. You're no party animal but have strong family values, a dependable nature and you still know how to have fun.

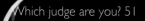

Bruno Tonioli

As Strictly's most effusive judge, Bruno Tonioli has raved over many a sexy salsa and cooed over his fair share of fabulous foxtrots. But the bouncy Italian has no time to remember past glories when a fresh bunch of potential Fred and Gingers are waiting in the wings.

'I never look back because with each launch we start again, just like you do in the Olympics,' he explains. 'The show progresses every season and we always want to do better than we did before.

'If you see the difference between dances that were performed on season one or two, compared to now, it's amazing how much they have evolved. But I, for one, expect it to evolve. If the last series was good I want to see better – and I'm pretty sure this year will be the best ever.'

What do you think of the line-up?

They are brilliant, a really interesting bunch. There are great characters. Gorgeous girls – Daisy Lowe, Laura Whitmore and Louise are all stunning. Tameka is a spice girl, a real hot chilli pepper with a great personality. Lesley Joseph is going to be brilliant. I can't tell how well she will dance but she will be plenty of fun.

How will the two Olympians do?

It's always good to have athletes straight from the success of the Olympics. We had them in 2012 and they bring a competitive streak to the series. They are used to winning and they have lots of energy. And Greg is a handsome man.

Did anyone surprise you in the launch show?

You can't tell much from the first group dance. You have to have a few shows before you can see how talented they are. It looks like a pretty competitive line-up.

Do you still get excited?

Yes, I do. And the moment I stop getting excited, I will stop doing it!

What did you think of last year's final?

This show progresses every season so I never look back because with each launch we always start all over again, with a whole new bunch of talent. You always want to do better than you did before and it's amazing how much the show has evolved so I'm pretty sure this year will be better than ever.

Which celebrity are you most excited about?

Will is a very interesting performer. He is very intelligent and always has great ideas, so he and Karen will come up with compelling routines.

Who do you think has potential?

With this lot it's impossible as they've all got potential.

Apart from Will and Daisy, Louise is a great performer, Danny looks like he could be very good and, judging by the early signs, Ore, Melvin, Naga and Laura all have a bit of rhythm. There is a lot of great potential. It may end in disaster but on paper they look pretty good to me.

Will Judge Rinder give Craig some lip?

Judge Rinder is taking this very seriously and he will put a lot of work into it. He's not there for a laugh but he is a very smart man. He isn't going to take any flack – and good for him! It's great to see somebody give back if comments are out of proportion.

STRICTLY
comes to
TOWN

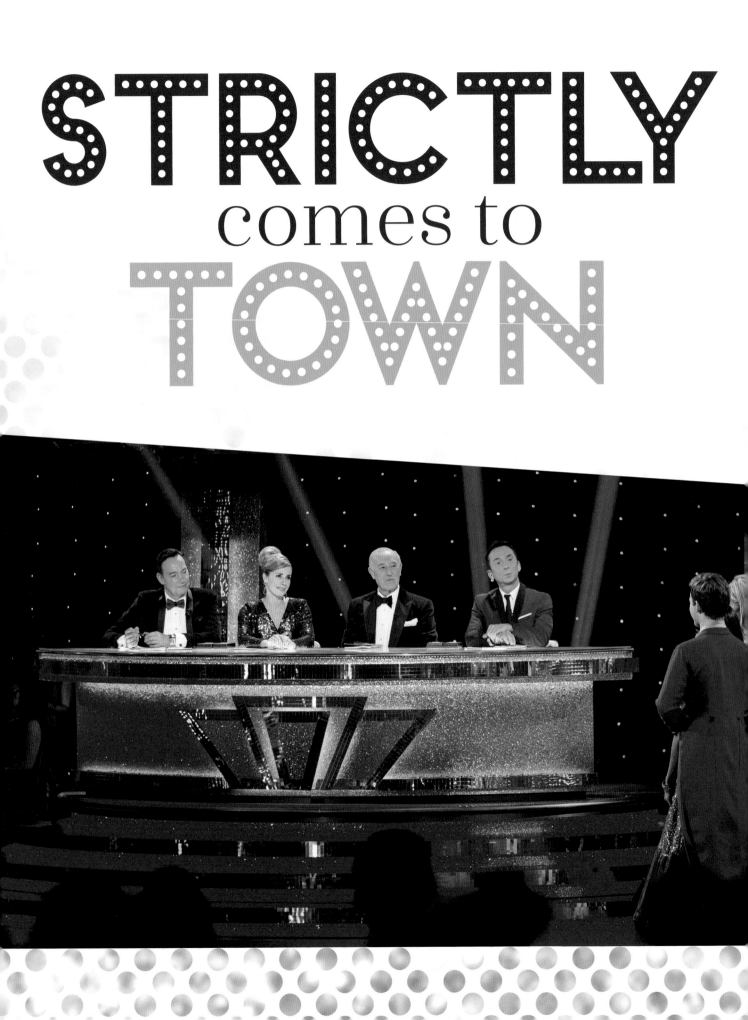

The Tower Ballroom was the venue for the show's precursor Come Dancing, and has since played host to two Strictly finals in 2004 and 2011, as well as providing the benchmark show that the competing couples aspire to reach.

For manager Kate Shane and her team, the annual arrival is an exciting event and planning is everything. With events running right up until the weekend before, the Tower team don't have much time to get the building ready for the Strictly invasion.

'The last event before Strictly finishes on midnight on Sunday so we have a big overnight clean and strip the room.

'We get rid of our furniture and clear it all back so it's ready for the arrival of the camera rig, the light fittings and the sound equipment. We take out an internal window at the back of the ballroom so the crew can run all the camera cables. We take out handrails on stairs so they can get the equipment in, then we get the dressing rooms ready.

'On Monday production arrive and on Tuesday, the articulated lorries come loaded with gear, with more and more arriving all week. They take over the whole building and every single space is filled with boxes and cases, because you can't travel light on a big show like this.

'The area we call the silver landing looks like a fairy grotto because there's loads of glittery fabric being cut up.'

In the ballroom the sprung dance floor has to be prepared. 'The springs can be adjusted to make it more of a solid dance floor and we tighten the back third, where the cameras sit, because you want minimum movement, but we still have it sprung where everyone is dancing.'

The show's set dressers then take over and drape the halls with sparkling fabrics, shiny props and tiny twinkling lights. 'It is a beautiful room anyway,' says Kate. 'And then it has that Strictly magic dust sprinkled all over it.'

'The silver landing looks like a fairy grotto because there's loads of glittery fabric being cut up.'

Set designer Patrick Doherty is in charge of the ballroom bling and his task is to maintain the beauty of the building while mirroring the familiar surrounds of the Strictly studio. The key to his transformation is in the LED lighting.

'There is a massive amount of LED ribbon that covers the existing stairs and turns them into a low-res screen, which we can put graphics on to,' he reveals. 'We put in further stairs and arches which are also covered in LED ribbon and the marble columns are covered by glitter columns with LED all the way round, then there are further elements for the entrances.

'We put a huge screen on the back wall, which replaces the painted backdrop and becomes our main screen backdrop, and the graphics on there are reflected in all the LED ribbons.'

The lower part of the ballroom is then draped in acres of starcloth, which twinkles with built-in lights and, in one corner, a temporary Clauditorium is built on a low platform.

Above The Clauditorium is reconstructed in the ballroom but without the famous stairs for the couples to run up

Above the historic dance floor goes a huge lighting rig, complete with extra chandeliers which are actually designed for the tour and borrowed by us for Blackpool, plus the obligatory mirror balls.

'We have restrictions at Blackpool

because everything has to fit through the doorways into the building, and they're less than two metres wide. Anything bigger has to come in bits and be built inside the venue and, once it's built, it has to be stored inside.

'If you were to look away from the main screen, you'd see a whole lot of massive props with drapes all over them being hidden from the audience.'

For the celebs and the pros, the annual pilgrimage to Blackpool is one of the highlights of the series.

'It's like Disneyworld for dancers,' says Karen Clifton. 'That ballroom is so special and you do feel like princes and princesses. There is magic in there and we create even more magic when we're on that dance floor with the lights and the dresses. It's a very exciting feeling.'

Natalie Lowe agrees: 'This is so regal and we're absolutely spoilt to perform on a beautiful sprung floor like this. We're rehearsing with massive smiles on our faces but once you get an audience in there and the judges and the lights, it really is a fairy tale.'

Above Choreographer Jason Gilkison and the dancers have just two days to perfect the group numbers in the venue

The hair and make-up rooms are smaller in the Blackpool venue but there's always room for everyone

that's amazing. It's twice the amount of audience from the TV studio and it's very exciting.'

For manager Kate Shane the Strictly weekend feels just like Christmas.

'This weekend is probably the most self-indulgent I get. I love the show, and just being part of this is incredible. It's such a buzz.

'The day after always feels a bit like Boxing Day blues. On the Sunday, when I come in and clear up, and we put that last bit of glitter in a bin bag, it's a bit sad. Twelve months to wait until the next time. We absolutely love it.'

For Kevin Clifton, who grew up in Grimsby, Blackpool holds special memories as he and sister Joanne competed in the national competitions here as children.

'It's been in my life since I was a kid and our whole year was geared towards dancing at Blackpool,' he recalls. 'There's a special magic about it, knowing the history of ballroom dancing here, and not just in competitions but in social dancing as well. For decades it's been the home of ballroom so it feels like Blackpool is made for this.' For the competing celebrities it is often the benchmark they set themselves at the start of the series. 'Everyone asks "Do you want to get to Blackpool?" about three weeks before,' laughs Kellie Bright. 'I just wanted to think about getting through to the next week! But it's a really special thing and it's something we the celebs take away with us. We got to dance at Blackpool and

Kate Shane loves the annual arrival of the *Strictly* crew

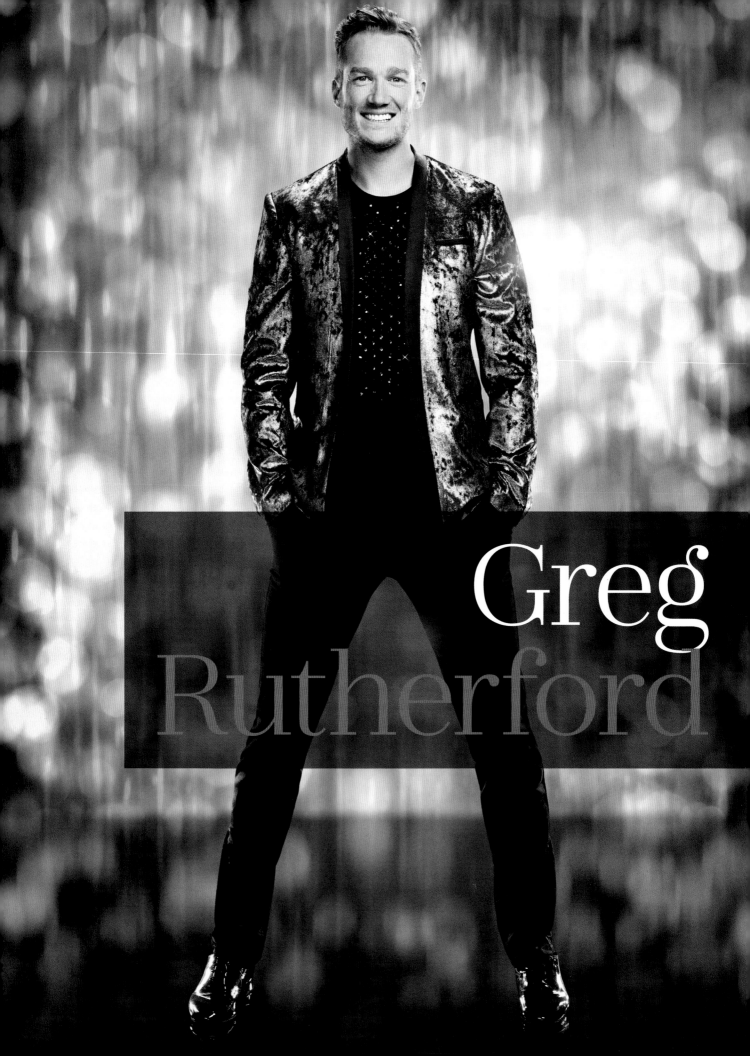

Greg
Rutherford

Olympian Greg Rutherford is fresh from Rio and hoping to add another prize to his heaving trophy cabinet. But, while he's a novice on the dance floor, the champion long jumper has a secret weapon at home – even if it is proving to be a double-edged sword.

'My partner Susie was a dancer until she was about 20 and she's very good,' he reveals. 'While I was training for the launch show, I sent the video of us training to Susie and, from the time I got into the car to when I got home, she'd learnt the dance, and was taking me through the dance steps and telling me where I was going wrong. And she looked fantastic doing it. I was thinking "You did that in an hour! I've spent days trying to get this right and I'm still awful."

'So in one way it's been an advantage because we can practise all weekend but the flipside is that I can now see how bad I am.'

The current world record holder for outdoors and indoors long jump, the 29-year-old athlete landed a gold medal at the 2012 Olympics before bagging a bronze at this year's Rio games. But 'throwing some shapes' in dance training has left him a little out of his comfort zone.

'I am truly not a dancer so this is a massive rude awakening for me,' he says.

'I can throw something but I'm not sure that you'd class them as actual shapes.

'It's been an eye-opener and it could be a very difficult process, but good fun.

'It's an interesting contrast because I want to improve and do well but there's another half of me that is coming into the competition saying "I'm not here to win. I'm here to learn the basics, last more than the first week and then I'll be gone." I'm happy to accept that, because there are people here who can dance.'

So which style is the Buckingham boy most keen to master?

'Just a dance, any dance, would be nice,' he laughs. 'It would be nice to be able to dance a bit with Susie and be able to formulate some sort of movement that looks like dance, instead of a drunken spider.'

After years spent in sportswear, Greg says he is not afraid of Lycra and is ready to embrace the sparkles. He is even happy to face the judges.

'That's the bit I'm looking forward to more than anything else,' he reveals. 'Everybody tells you you're doing great all the time, but I will finally get the real perception of what's going on when I face the judges. I'm used to criticism because that's the world I come from. They tell you you're bad in order to get you to improve and when you've done well they say nothing, so for me that will be a great help.'

Natalie Lowe

Dancer Natalie Lowe jumped at the chance to partner Olympian Greg Rutherford for this series as she has a passion for athletics. In the first week of training, she went to watch the long jumper in action at his final event of the year, in Newcastle.

'It's nice to see the mechanics of everything and how his body works, where his power is,' she says. 'I find it fascinating. I loved athletics growing up and if I wasn't dancing I'd be doing athletics. I was school champion four years in a row, and I loved long jump, high jump and the 100-metre sprint, so we have that in common.'

The Australian dancer had her eye on Greg as a potential dance partner before they were paired.

'He's six foot two and he has an amazing work ethic – what Olympian doesn't?' she explains. 'So I feel honoured and excited about experiencing as much as we can together and just being the best we can be. It's going to be an interesting journey and I'm looking forward to it.'

Natalie is not giving the gold medallist an easy transition into the world of dance. 'We are planning to come out with a bang,' she said. 'I'm not holding back so I feel a bit sorry for him because I'm throwing him in at the deep end. It's so foreign to what he does – what he calls "running forwards into a sandpit" – and he has never danced a day in his life. So it's challenging but I think he will "jump" to the occasion!'

Despite being a complete novice Greg is putting in the hours, says his tutor.

'He is very determined and he is going to not stop until he gets it,' she says. 'He has an amazing attitude and that's all I ask for, someone who will graft until they get it right, or as right as they can. We're also having a load of fun in the studio. We can't stop laughing.'

Last year saw Natalie, now in her eighth Strictly series, cooking up some tasty routines with TV chef Ainsley Harriott. Sadly, they only made it to the fifth week but she had a blast.

'Ainsley was fab,' she says. 'He's a beam of energy. He only had to go out and smile and he lit up everybody's living rooms.

While Natalie is hoping Greg will impress all the judges with his moves, she admits she is especially keen to please Len.

'I'm gutted it's his last series,' she says. 'He's had an amazing run, but I was devastated when I found out. I even shed a tear. The final is going to be so emotional so on this series, I'm dancing for Len!'

Strictly BLACKPOOL

The spacious opulence of the Tower Ballroom provides the perfect backdrop for Strictly's most dramatic costumes.

While the couples relish the bigger dance floor, the quirky, higgledy-piggledy nature of the backstage area means limited space for the production departments. Designer Vicky Gill and her team are tucked at the back of the ballroom down a steep, winding staircase in a small narrow room, beavering away on the final alterations.

With two group dances, a musical number and extra dancers joining the eight remaining couples, there are over 120 outfits for the costume department to create for the Blackpool extravaganza. 'Last week, we talked to all the dancers to make sure we come up with outfits that they're happy with,' Vicky explains.

'On most weeks, I can absorb major changes at the last minute but in Blackpool we need that to be at a minimum because

Above The long, thin costume department at the Blackpool Tower is a hive of activity on Saturday morning

there's so much to do.'

To get to the ballroom on time, the costumes need to be ready and delivered to Elstree studios a day earlier than usual, on Wednesday night. By 8 a.m. on Thursday they are packed in a lorry and on the road, while the team travel up by train, leaving Vicky to finish off the final pieces and drive up on Friday morning. A few items from the high street are added to the custom-made costumes, but that doesn't mean they are used straight off the peg.

'We're not cutting and sewing as many outfits, but we still have to fit them, make sure the shoulders won't lift out as the dancer moves and it all works,' says Vicky. 'If we haven't done that in the prep, we're doing it here on Friday and Saturday.

'Plus every dress will need something done, from an alteration to a tweak, because that's the nature of the outfits.'

A glance around the temporary costume department is an instant demonstration of that. Two of the girls, Amy and Lauren, are painstakingly gluing crystals to one of the outfits for a little extra Strictly sparkle, Vicky's assistant Theresa is helping with Jamelia's final fitting of a stunning blue and pink ballgown, and seamstress Michelle is working on a beautiful red dress with a sparkling mesh top and flowing skirt for Anita Rani's paso.

'I'm trying to get a colour palette across the entire show, so I have to allocate colour depending on the concepts,' explains Vicky. 'That means that not every dancer can

Below Anita Rani's stunning paso dress gets the finishing touches just before the Friday rehearsal

have the same colour. Originally, we had two pasos so we had to hold fire on the costume until the final decision was made.

'In Anita and Gleb's number there's a silk hanging down from the ceiling that tucks into the back of her dress, so we had to see the silk before we could finish. We see videos of the routine, but sometimes you need to see the actual thing to know exactly what you're doing.

'Anita has a circular skirt on top of the dress, with quick release Velcro so she can pull away. It will look very dramatic.'

Even in this hive of activity there is

Above The *Countryfile* presenter ditches the wellies for the glamorous gown as she takes to the floor in Blackpool

time for a giggle. Cackles of laughter can be heard as Tristan MacManus tries on his flat cap and braces for the group dance and breaks into an Irish jig, and dancers and celebs are constantly popping in for a last-minute fitting and a chat.

'It's a lot more hectic than usual but we always get through it and somehow pull it off,' says Vicky. 'And it's always tons of fun.'

Laura Whitmore

Having grown up in Ireland, Laura Whitmore is no stranger to dancing at family get-togethers and says her mum and her sisters do a mean jive.

But her description of her own dancing prowess is less than complimentary.

'I'm all right on the dance floor,' she reveals. 'But I'm a bit like Bambi on ice, limbs everywhere.

'I love dancing but I've never learned how to dance professionally and I'm a huge Strictly fan so I've always wanted to do it. When can you ever get an experience like this? Getting the opportunity to learn so much from professional dancers in such a small space of time is amazing.'

The TV presenter comes from a huge family and her mum is one of 13, so she'll have quite a crowd cheering her on in her hometown of Bray, County Wicklow. She's also expecting to see a few familiar faces in the Strictly studio.

'My mum, my aunties, my friend's granny – everyone wants to come,' laughs Laura. 'There are going to be a few extra planes flying over from Ireland. It's crazy the wide range of ages who love the show. My godson is only four and he is going to fly over, even though he's too young to come to the show but he is going to come to watch me rehearse.'

The 31-year-old TV host is enjoying dressing up for the dances.

'I was a bit scared to start with,' she says. 'I'm used to dressing up for red carpets but this is totally different stuff. When you put it on you suddenly become a totally different character.'

Laura has fronted the ITV show *I'm a Celebrity, Get Me Out of Here! Now!* for the last five years, after taking over from Caroline Flack. But can she follow in the former Strictly champ's footsteps one more time.

'Don't compare me to Caroline Flack!' she laughs. 'People have asked me which friends have done the show and it's Caroline, Alesha Dixon – everyone I know did really well.

'But I'm not thinking about the trophy yet. I just want to learn how to dance. It's a specific skill that not everyone gets the opportunity to learn so I'm going to make the most of it.'

One thing the blonde presenter is looking forward to is the spray tan.

'I'm Irish,' she explains. 'I used to spend two months in Australia and still come back paler than most people!'

Giovanni
Pernice

'Being on Strictly was my dream already and getting into the final was even more so,' he reveals. 'When you get to the final, of course you want to win. But Georgia was an amazing partner and, at the end of the day, we really wanted to stay in the competition until the last day and do all the dances. So we are happy with that.'

The Sicilian, who took up ballroom after watching *Come Dancing* as a child, moved to Bologna at 14 to study dance and trained alongside fellow Strictly pro Joanne Clifton. He won numerous championships including the 2012 Italian title, which inspired a tattoo on his arm with the date and the words 'Nato Per Vincere' or 'Born to Win.'

In his second year on the show, Giovanni is paired with TV presenter Laura Whitmore, and he has no complaints.

'I had seen Laura dancing a little bit and she can dance, so I was happy,' he says. 'Our first rehearsals have gone really well, plus she has lots of personality and we are going to play a lot with that. She is also confident – which helps. Happy days!'

While leggy Laura describes her dancing style as 'Bambi on ice', Giovanni believes long limbs needn't be a disadvantage.

'It can be a problem because long legs can be difficult for a dancer,' he says. 'But if you use them the right way, they can be an advantage. So if you do a perfect straight leg or bent leg, it can look great but if you make a mistake, even a small one, it is really noticeable. So let's hope she does it right.'

It won't be for want of trying, if reports from her new tutor are anything to go by.

'Laura concentrates on the dance and puts all her energy into it, and that's all I'm asking for. My job is to teach her how to dance and as long as she is focused and enthusiastic, that's all I need.'

Although he admits there is stiff competition for the final this year, Giovanni feels Laura could be an all-rounder when it comes to the dance styles.

She's sassy and confident which will be good in Latin but she can also be elegant which will work in the ballroom. 'So hopefully she will be good at both of them. And I'll be quite happy about that.'

TEN YEARS
on tour

When the champion's trophy has been handed out and the last grain of glitter has been swept from the studio floor, it's not all over for Strictly fans. The celebs want to 'Keeeep dancing' and the Live Tour means they can spread that Strictly sparkle a little bit further.

This year, the Strictly Come Dancing Live Tour celebrates its tenth outing with over 30 dates in venues around the UK.

'This year we're going to go for broke because it's our tenth year,' promises Fiona Pearce, Creative Director at Stage Entertainment, who produces the Live Tour. 'It's going to be bigger and better than ever before.'

To date the Live Tour has sold over two million tickets. with many superfans turning up at three or four shows in one year.

'The live show is exciting because it's a different experience for the audience,' says Fiona. 'We make it as spectacular as we can, while sticking to the format of the TV show, and the audience can see the incredible dancing live – it's a fantastic experience.'

Putting on the glitz

Planning for the Live Tour begins in May with initial designs first on the agenda. 'It is an homage to the TV show but it is also live entertainment so you have to make sure you have a good range of people and appeal to everyone,' Fiona says. 'They're not necessarily just the best dancers.'

The Live Tour also works hard to replicate the award-winning production values of the TV show, including the themes, set design and group dances.

Rehearsals for the Live Tour begin in the first week of the New Year. 'We have an intense rehearsal week in London in January,' explains tour manager Tony Harpur. 'We then go to Birmingham, where we kick off, and we have from Tuesday to

Friday for technical rehearsals. There's a lot to do and usually there's a technical challenge or two. Last year, for example, we had an aerial performer in the air in a large ring so there's always something new to be factored in.'

Moving between arenas, often with less than 24 hours between shows, is a huge operation. The motors – rigging that holds up the lights etc. – will go into the venue the night before but everything else is done on the day.

'We start with a bare arena,' reveals technical director Andy Gibbs. 'If we're doing an evening show, we start at 7 a.m. and we'll be ready for a sound check at 4 p.m. The toughest turnaround is when we go from Wembley, where we have an evening show on Friday, and take it to The O2 for a matinee the next day. We start at 6 a.m. to be ready for 2.30 p.m. so we have less than seven hours. We've got a system that works in the venues we go back to, year after year.'

Andy's team of 50 crew travels with 16 trucks full of equipment and, on the day, another team of 60 local workers is brought in to help.

'We have 1,200 panels to make up the dance floor, which measures 40 metres by 20 metres,' explains Andy. 'There's a stage with the Strictly steps for the dancers to come down, where the band are, then you need lights, sound and video equipment and the famous mirror ball, and we take all of that with us. We've had the same two-metre mirror ball since the start so this will be its tenth year on tour.'

In terms of performance space, the show is one of the biggest the arenas have housed.

'A stage for a rock band would be about the size that we just use for the judges and band, then we have three times that in

To date over two million people have visited the Strictly Come Dancing Live Tour.

The Tour has travelled over 10,000 miles and given 300 performances.

Over 60 celebrities have performed.

additional space,' says Tony. 'It's a big stage.'

With 130 cast and crew, staging 31 shows in under five weeks, organisation is everything and Tony and Andy have it timed to a T.

'I work with Andy to make sure schedules make sense, that we're on the same page,' says Tony. 'With so many people, one tiny delay can disrupt the whole system.'

Over the last decade, the Live Tour has grown in size and is now more spectacular than ever.

'The TV show has become bigger and better and that helps keep the Tour fresh,' says Fiona Pearce. 'We include big show pieces, the big stage numbers which showcase the abilities of all the dancers.'

'There is nothing like standing at the back of an arena watching 10,000 people enjoying a show that you and all your team have spent the best part of a year putting together. It's fabulous.'

Ballroom bitz

Four buses and 16 articulated lorries take the artists and the set around the country.

1,200 floor panels are laid to make the biggest dance floor in the country.

There are 225 lights, eight chandeliers and nine massive mirror balls.

The catering team provides 1,470 breakfasts (and cooks 2,100 sausages), 1,470 lunches and 3,240 dinners on tour.

There are over 100 costumes – each with matching shoes, jewellery and accessories.

A ballroom dress takes up to 10 metres of fabric, plus embellishment and trimmings.

Each dress can have up to 10,000 crystals, all applied by hand.

Lesley Joseph

Comedy star Lesley Joseph has a list of reasons for wanting to sign up to Strictly Come Dancing.

'It's one of the most iconic – if not the most iconic – programmes on television,' she explains. 'It's fun, it's escapism, it's glamorous and I want a spray tan. I love the show and I could not say no. Oh, and I want to learn to dance!'

The London-born actress has become a household name since taking on the role of the outrageous Dorien Green in *Birds of a Feather* 27 years ago. The comedy – which also stars Linda Robson and Pauline Quirke – is currently enjoying a revival and Lesley says her fellow 'Birds' will be flocking together to cheer her on during her run on Strictly.

'Pauline and Linda came to the launch show and they are over the moon, completely and absolutely thrilled. Linda, especially, is beside herself with joy.'

The TV legend, now 70, has been limbering up for the show with a busy exercise regime and wants to make sure she is in peak shape for the live shows.

'I think my biggest challenge will probably be the physicality of it all,' she admits. 'I've been trying to do lots of cardio stuff so I am walking everywhere plus doing exercise classes and yoga classes as much as I can and trying to lose weight but I am failing in that so far!

'I think another challenge will be trying to keep going with the training. I'm not 21, I'm not 31 or 41 so I think as far as that's concerned that will probably be the biggest challenge. I want to be able to pace myself and not absolutely exhaust myself before I get to Saturday night.'

Lesley promises to be a keen student and wants to make it through the early rounds of the competition so partner Anton can teach her as many dances as possible.

'There are some dances that I really would love to do, especially the Charleston and the cha-cha,' she says. 'I'd love to do some of the Latin dances so I would feel slightly cheated if I only got to a chance to do the waltz. It's not a question of wanting to go further in the competition so much as getting to do more dances.

'Even so, I have to say I would love to get to Blackpool because the Tower Ballroom is one of the most beautiful ballrooms in the world, and it would be such an honour to dance there.'

Anton
Du Beke

Since very first tentative steps were taken on Strictly Come Dancing, Anton Du Beke has been entertaining audiences with his witty routines.

Along with such partners as Judy Murray, Jerry Hall, Nancy Dell'Olio, Ann Widdecombe and Katie Derham he has provided many of the most memorable dances in the show's history.

Last year Anton and Radio 3 and Proms presenter Katie Derham waltzed into fourth place.

'You're with each other for a long time every day and Katie was a joy to be with,' he says. 'She actually turned out to be rather good so that was a little added bonus for me, but I enjoy dancing with all my partners, be it Ann Widdecombe or Judy Murray.'

Anton grew up in Sevenoaks, Kent with his Spanish mother, Hungarian father, and his brother and sister. A talented junior boxer and county footballer, he came to dancing at the relatively late age of 14, when his contemporaries were already well established on the junior circuit. He studied contemporary, jazz, ballet and modern theatre dance until, inspired by his idol Fred Astaire, he decided to specialise in ballroom. His favourite dance has always been the foxtrot because, he says, 'It's a proper dance with proper music.'

In 1997, Anton met Erin Boag, and within a year they had captured the New Zealand Championship – a feat they repeated the following year. After seven years of competing, they both joined Strictly for the first series in 2004.

In 2010, despite consistently low marks, Ann and Anton captured the public's imagination and made it all the way to the quarter-final. One legendary routine saw Ann fly in over the stage to the dance floor, prompting Bruno to name her 'Starship Widdecombe'.

'I've been the luckiest of the professional dancers by having the most interesting and lovely ladies to dance with over the years,' Anton says. 'If I hadn't danced with Ann Widdecombe that would have been my loss because she was a joy – such a scream and fun to be with.'

This year Anton is partnered with *Birds of a Feather* star Lesley Joseph – and he hopes to fly into the final again.

'She's doing incredibly well,' says Anton. 'I'm amazed it's this good. She's pulling off the figures nicely. A double reverse spin on the first day. Boom!'

For her part, she is looking forward to the more dramatic dances with the Strictly stalwart.

'This man is iconic, a legend,' she says. 'And I can't wait for Halloween.'

FLIGHTS
of
FANCY

From Ann Widdecombe's 'flying fortress' tango to Georgia May Foote wistfully perched on a moon, many a Strictly routine has got off to a flying start. Recent dances have included a giant surfboard, ridden by Frankie Bridge and Kevin Clifton, a magic carpet and even Chitty Chitty Bang Bang taking to the skies.

Stringing him along … Craig Revel Horwood makes a noteworthy entrance on a huge guitar in Blackpool

Behind these moments of magic are two men, Erland 'Spider' Webb and Jared Doughty of DLM Events, and a whole lot of heavy machinery that fills an 18-tonne truck and has to be installed every week.

'It's a good day's work to get a rig in for a show,' explains Erland. 'We put a tracking system in with two winches: one for the vertical movement and one for the horizontal. The track goes in a straight line, from where we start from and fly to. If it's one person flying we use a smaller system, but if we're doing the big props, like the cars or the surfboard, we put in a heavy-duty system to take more weight.'

The dancers and celebs are safely secured for every airborne activity. If sitting or standing on a prop, a quick-release waist belt is used, but the heavier harnesses, used for flying solo, present their own issues. 'You can't dance in a harness,' reveals Erland. 'So we have to rush on and take the harnesses off. The performer comes down at the start and the camera will turn on to the professional dancer for 10 seconds while we unclip them, then we run out of shot before they dance.'

Any dancer taking to the air has a special flying rehearsal on Thursday night before attempting the entrance in the

Georgia May Foote looked heavenly as she floated
on a crescent moon over the dance floor

Above Right Acrobatic dancer
Jasmine adds a touch of the
flying circus to the show in
Blackpool and the tour

Friday rehearsals. But Erland reveals it's easier than it looks.

'In most of the harnesses they will naturally find a position they can hold and then we do the rest, lifting and dropping them using the computer system. All they have to do is sit there and look pretty.

'The flying mustn't be a big part of the routine because it's all about the dancing, so it has to be a slick effect that isn't going to distract anybody.'

While the pro dancers come up with the routines, the celebs are consulted about any fears before flying is considered. 'A few of them are nervous, but by the time they do this sort of thing they've conquered so many fears they're up for it,' says Erland. 'We wouldn't put anyone up there who was scared of heights.'

Silks and circus acts

One fearless flyer in the Strictly team is Jasmine Takacs. This incredible dancer can often be found suspended from silks in the air while performing acrobatic dance moves. It's a skill she first showcased on the *Strictly Come Dancing* Live Tour before bringing it one the main show in Blackpool.

Amazingly, Jasmine learned her circus skills in one afternoon – the day before the first tour show.

'Four days before the tour, choreographer Jason Gilkison and *Strictly Come Dancing* Live Tour Director Craig Revel Horwood asked me if I could go up in the silks. I thought I'd give it a go so I called around some circus friends and found a teacher who was free on Sunday, our day off. I said, "See what you can do with me in three hours." 'She was shocked but agreed, and thankfully I have a strong back and

arms – so I had no problem lifting myself up and was soon climbing like a monkey.'

Although not recommended for the amateur, Jasmine had a natural advantage.

'I lift weights in the gym to keep strong and prevent injury, and that has a huge benefit. My teacher said that in the first year most people just build the strength to pull themselves up but I already did pull ups and chin ups.

'It's all in the back strength and the momentum of getting the feet right. If you're tired and you begin to lose your grip, it's a bit scary but I feel pretty secure. I'm in control.'

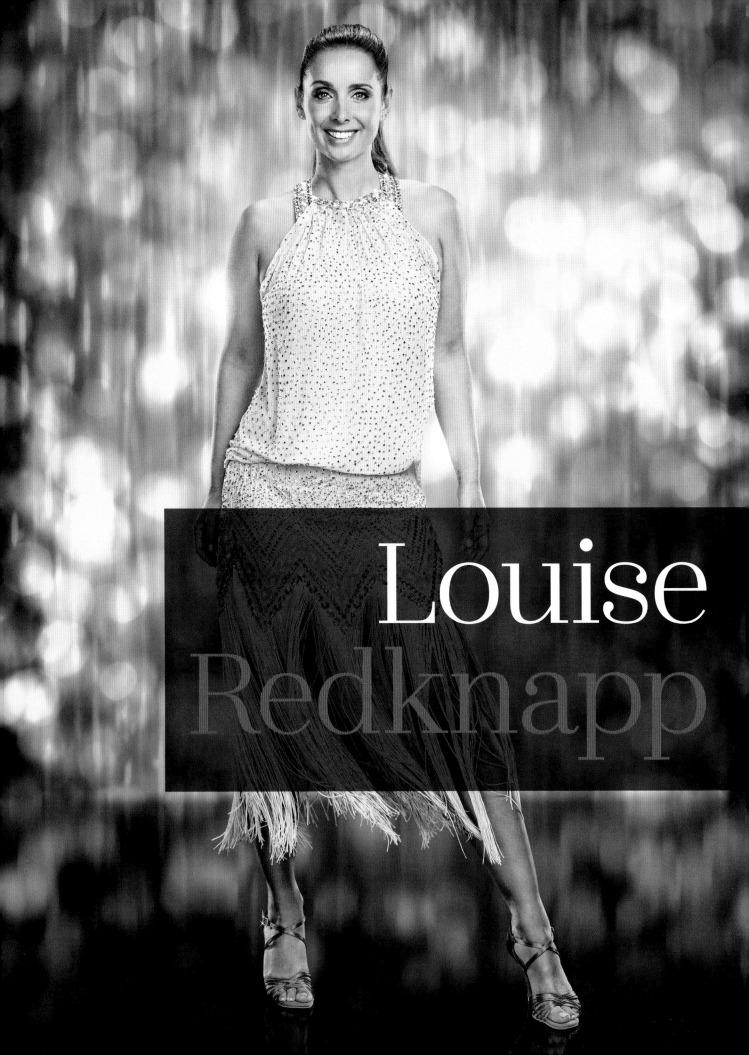

Louise
Redknapp

Having shot to fame in the 1990s as a member of the chart-topping girl group Eternal, Louise Redknapp has some dance experience under her belt. But she admits it's been a while since she broke out her best moves.

'I did music a long time ago so I honestly don't know how much of a help it's going to be until I start learning the proper routines,' she says. 'For me the hurdle is going to be putting it all into action.

'In a pop video, you have dancers who make you look really good and everything is completely tailored to what works for you so they don't give you a hard routine. They choreograph what you are good at, and you do a lot of that through your song. If you forget it you just walk it and clap and join in again later.'

Louise was just 16 when she formed Eternal with Kéllé Bryan and sisters Easther and Vernie Bennett. At 21, she left to pursue a solo career, producing three platinum albums and selling over 15 million records. In 1998, she married footballer Jamie Redknapp and the couple have two children: Charley, 12, and seven-year-old Beau.

'The timing was key to my decision to do Strictly,' she says. 'I was asked before but Beau was still a toddler and I couldn't give it the time it needed to not embarrass myself. Now, both the boys are off doing their football, they're with their dad a lot so I thought I deserved to have a little bit of time back for me now, just for a few weeks.'

The 41-year-old, who was born in south London, says husband Jamie will be supporting her through her Strictly journey. 'Initially, I think Jamie was nervous because he's used to me being at home and being the core of the household,' she reveals. 'At the same time we've never lived in each other's pockets. I've never been that wife that's been at every football match and vice versa with Jamie and my gigs. He said, "I think it will be great for you to go and do something for you. Go and smash it."'

Louise is keen to show her family what she can do on the dance floor.

'Jamie hasn't seen me dance for years but when we met, I danced,' she says. 'I'm quite looking forward to him seeing me like that again and remembering that's what I did, and I wasn't always a stay-at-home mum. I think it will be good for all of us.

'Being boys, Charley and Beau are quite impressed with their dad and not particularly their mum. They'll probably be a little bit embarrassed but I do want to make them proud.'

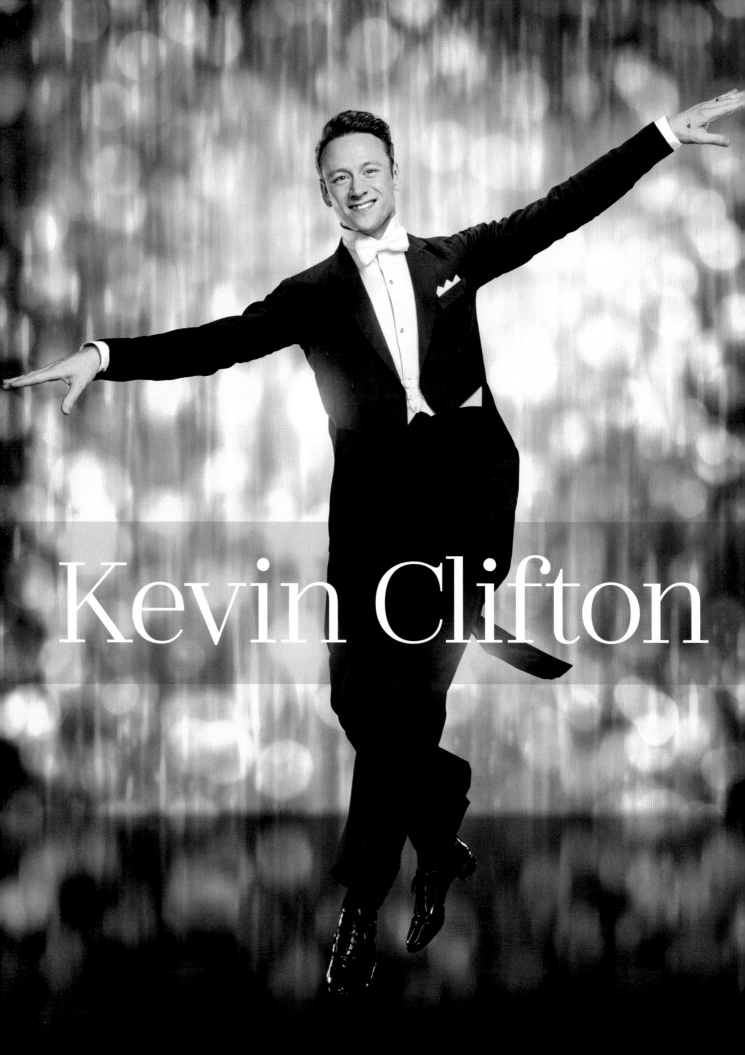

Kevin Clifton

'It would be lovely, of course,' he admits. 'But I'm wary of putting that pressure on Louise. I don't want her to worry that she might be the first one to not go to the final with Kevin. I keep reminding her that it doesn't matter what round it is, because we need to take it week by week and do the best we can on that particular day. I'm focusing on that and not thinking about the final.'

Kevin and his sister, fellow Strictly-pro Joanne, grew up in the world of ballroom, being taught by parents, former World Champions Keith and Judy Clifton. He became Youth World Number 1 and four-time British Latin Champion, as well as winning International Opens in numerous countries and rising to the rank of seventh in the world.

In 2013, the Grimsby lad joined wife Karen Clifton on Strictly and shot to the final with Susanna Reid, repeating the feat the following year with Frankie Bridge and then Kellie Bright.

'Frankie lives two doors away from Louise and they're good friends,' he reveals. 'When the celebrities were announced she sent me a text saying "Louise is a really nice girl so it would be amazing if you got her." Because of that I really wanted Louise – which is why I lost control on the launch show a little bit!'

That's not the only reason Kevin is thrilled to be partnering the former Eternal star. As a huge football fan, he was quite excited to meet her partner, Jamie Redknapp.

'Jamie came in on the first day of rehearsals and at first I thought he wouldn't be much interested in the dancing but he got really into it and then he started asking all the right questions.

'Although I try and play it cool when he's in the room, he's one of the biggest names in football so it was exciting for me.'

Kevin is also happy with the work ethic of his new pupil.

'She's so lovely to work with so I'm really enjoying it,' he says. 'She's eager to get it right and she told me, "I want you to push me. Don't let me get away with anything!" So I've been really pushing her and giving her some really difficult stuff but she loves it so I'm really hopeful.'

Melvin
Odoom

DJ Melvin Odoom is more used to spinning discs than spinning around the dance floor but he is looking forward to taking on the Latin numbers. The more elegant dances, however, could be a different matter.

'The hardest for me will be the ballroom,' he admits. 'My posture is so bad and I'm not used to standing that way. We did a little taster in the first week and I found that quite difficult, so that's something I really need to work on.

'But everyone is so cool, and the professional dancers are so patient so it's a great atmosphere and we're learning a new skill, and learning it for free! I don't have to go to dance classes.'

Being a complete novice, Melvin admits he was a surprised by the dancing skills of his fellow contestants after training with them for the first group dance.

'I was thinking, "There's going to be some rubbish people we can get rid of first." But after the first routine I thought, "Everyone is good." The opening dance at the launch show showed it is going to be a great series.'

The former *Xtra Factor* presenter, who co-hosts Kiss 100's breakfast show with Rickie Haywood Williams and Charlie Hedges, has plenty of support from family, friends and fans.

'My mum's one of Strictly's biggest fans so I'm really popular in my house at the moment,' he laughs. 'I'm the golden boy – just for now. Once it's over my sister will be number one again!

'Rickie thinks it's hilarious. He can't wait to see the outfits so he can laugh at me. But everywhere I go, Strictly's the only thing that anyone wants to speak to me about. I spent the weekend in Ibiza and Marbella and literally everyone I spoke to wanted to talk about nothing else. Everyone was wishing me good luck and asking me what I'd be wearing. It's a big show!'

Unlike many of his fellow contenders, Melvin is looking forward to coming up in front of the fearsome foursome.

'I can't wait to meet the judges,' he says. 'It's a big honour to be doing Len's last year and I'm glad I got on the show when he's still here.'

When it comes to putting on the sequins and sparkles, the 36-year-old promises he won't be shy.

'You can put me in anything,' he says. I don't mind what I wear as long as I can dance really well. I'll even shave my chest!'

Janette
Manrara

American dancer Janette is thrilled to be returning for her fourth series of Strictly, after what she calls 'three incredible years' on the show. But she admits that the wait to find out who she was paired with this year had her on the edge of her seat.

'The launch is the most nerve-racking episode because the person you get will shape the next four months of your life,' she explains. 'I thought I'd be laid-back by now but this is the fourth year and my nerves are getting worse.'

But pint-sized professional Janette – who is five foot without her dancing shoes – was thrilled to be paired with five foor four DJ Melvin Odoom.

'I was screaming for joy,' she reveals. 'I had my eye on him because it's awkward for me to do ballroom with men who are too tall. Last year, I had a great partner in Peter Andre but even he was slightly too tall. I'm just so small!'

The Florida-born firecracker, who is engaged to fellow pro Aljaž, wasn't the only one who was jumping for joy over the pairing.

'Melvin comes from a close-knit family and I met his parents and sister after the launch show. His mum is a huge fan of

Strictly and she said she was secretly hoping he would get me because of the height. She was also a fan of my past routines and loved watching me with Peter, so she was over the moon. That was really nice to hear.'

Although Melvin is a complete novice when it comes to dance training, Janette has already spotted some potential.

'I'm starting from scratch with him but he's very strong, he has rhythm and he can keep count. Plus he has the understanding of music because he's a DJ, so all those things are positive. He loves dancing when he's out, plus his personality is so big. He comes across as the funny one but in the little time I've spent with him, I've found he's just a really nice guy.'

But it's not all about winning for Janette. 'I want to have fun,' she says. 'I like to work hard, and get better but for me the priority is my celebrity, because this is the only time they will get to do Strictly. I want to enjoy myself and make sure my celebrity has a good time.

'My plan is to not focus on what everybody else is doing and to focus on us, hoping we make people smile, that we have fun and that we improve as the weeks go on. It's great to see your celebrity getting better because it makes you feel proud as a teacher.

'That's the game plan – one week at a time, and one routine at a time.'

PROM
date

The auditorium is swathed in blue light, an LED screen sparkles with special effects and a glitter ball hangs from the ceiling as the pros take to the floor. But this is not the studio on a Saturday night — it's the historical surroundings of the Royal Albert Hall and Strictly Come Dancing is about to get its very own Night at the Proms.

Aljaž and Janette have a ball as they take the stage at the Royal Albert Hall

In just a few hours, 5,000 fans will be filing through the door to watch six of the show's regulars – Kevin and Karen Clifton, Joanne Clifton, Giovanni Pernice, Aljaž Skorjanec and Janette Manrara – dance to two hours of music played by the BBC Concert Orchestra.

Above their heads, naturally, is the show's trademark spinning ball. 'The glitter ball was the first thing I noticed when I walked in,' laughs Janette. 'It follows us wherever we go.'

During the course of the show, each of the couples will dance two solo numbers as well as two group numbers – kicking off with a ballroom routine of almost six minutes to the overture from Gypsy. Prom presenter and Strictly finalist Katie Derham will bring the two worlds together by performing two dances, with Aljaž standing in for her Strictly partner Anton Du Beke. 'Each of the numbers tells a completely different story, which we love,' says Janette. 'There are so many characters and it's really beautiful.'

There is a buzz of excitement backstage as the dancers prepare for the first ever Strictly Prom.

'Karen and I were watching the prom last year and saying it would be great to go because it's such a good atmosphere,' recalls Kevin. 'A year later we're onstage here. This is a once-in-a-lifetime opportunity so I'm a little nervous but we're really excited.'

Kevin and sister Joanne are veterans

of the Albert Hall dance floor, having competed in international ballroom competitions when they were younger.

'When you think of all the performers who have been through here over the decades, it's a very special place,' says Kevin.'

Joanne adds: 'We used to do competitions here, where they take all the seating out of the middle to make a dance floor, but to be dancing on the stage with that massive orchestra, in front of 5,000 people, will be magical.'

For Giovanni, the venue is a new experience.

'It's the first time I've performed at the Royal Albert Hall and I'm really excited,' he reveals. 'It's a massive place and a huge orchestra which is amazing.'

Dancer Joanne returns to the home of her ballroom competitions in a blaze of glory

The 80-piece orchestra, conducted by Gavin Sutherland, adds a new dimension to the performances.

'The power of the music is beyond anything,' says Karen. 'I love music and there is nothing like dancing with an orchestra, driving your movement and your emotions. I feel like I'm in a movie.'

Timing is key to the live Prom and these running order notes are crucial

Aljaž and Janette said dancing to the live music in the final rehearsals made a huge difference.

'Dancing in front of this massive orchestra, probably one of the best in the world, is incredible,' says Aljaž. 'During the week we've been rehearsing to a recording, which is not the same but to get into the hall, with the orchestra, is wonderful.'

After a few days of prep with an assistant, choreographer Jason Gilkison has put all the routines together in just five days of rehearsals with the dancers.

'I knew we had a short window so I had everything mapped out for them when they came in on Sunday,' he explains. 'We had the opening number done by lunch.

We finished going through the routines on Monday evening.

'I feel so privileged. Although we had a short time, we all wanted it to be something special as if we'd been putting it together for months. On the first day we did ten hours and it was intense but nobody complained.'

In fact, all six professionals were taking it all in their beautifully placed stride.

'Jason is the best in the world and he's such a nice guy to work with,' says Giovanni. 'When you have a good choreographer and good dancers, it's not difficult to learn the dances quickly.'

'Jason is a genius,' says Kevin. 'He knows us well, he knows our strengths, and he

gets us on the same wavelength as him. He comes in with the idea, explains it to us and the dance takes form very quickly.'

The dancers catch up backstage after months apart

Craig Revel Horwood

In the year of the Rio Olympics, Craig Revel Horwood is keen to see two of Britain's best athletes – long jumper Greg Rutherford and gymnast Claudia Fragapane – hit the dance floor.

'As this is the Great Britain's best Olympics ever, the Olympians will have the whole nation behind them and it's a wonderful thing,' says the Australian-born judge. 'Greg won gold in 2012 and they both did so well in this year's games. So they are off to a good start and I think they'll be phenomenal.'

From the rest of the line-up Craig is expecting some stunning moves, a few laughs – and perhaps the odd spat with one or two of the feistier contestants.

'The new line-up is fantastic and this year is very different' he reveals.

Who is your 'one to watch'?
Danny Mac. He'll be a housewives' favourite and I think he's going to do really well. He has done some musical theatre and apparently he's really nice and very talented.

As a gymnast, Claudia Fragapane will be great at doing all the lifts and she'll have really good extensions, posture and rhythm. And because she's an athlete she will have that competitive streak and she's bound to work hard.

Who do you expect to be the most entertaining?
Ed Balls. He has the gift of the gab, and is very clever, and I think he'll be funny. Like Ann Widdecombe and John Sergeant, who were talented at public speaking, he will win the public over.

Are you expecting spats with Judge Rinder?
There will be sparring because we are very similar creatures. It'll be handbags at dawn. He's extremely competitive and he drives himself really hard physically, doing marathons and working out at the gym, so he's in good shape but I expect him to be feisty.

What did you think of last year's final?
The finalists were brilliant. I thought Jay McGuiness was great and I thought his week three jive was amazing. Kellie Bright did the most fantastic show dance, with Kevin, and I loved her. Georgia May Foote was adorable, like a little princess, which was wonderful for all the young female fans who looked up to her and wanted to dance like her. Anton made it into the final as well this year, which was great for him, and his partner Katie Derham was a very elegant dancer.

How do you feel about Len leaving?
I'll miss the sparring, and the telling me off and him pointing at me all the time. We'll all miss him but we wish him well and we'll try and make his final year amazing. No more pickled walnuts for us!

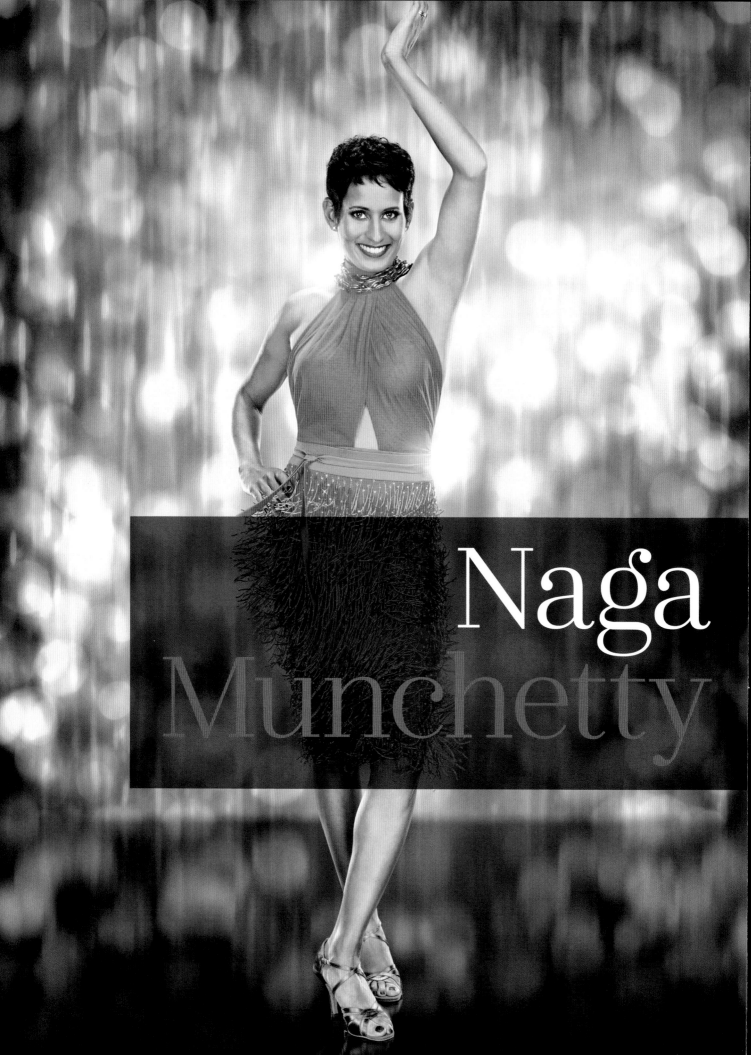

Naga
Munchetty

BBC viewers are more used to seeing Naga Munchetty sitting on a sofa than strutting her stuff on the dance floor. But the top-flight journalist is no couch potato – Naga plays golf around five times a week and recently won a prestigious cup at Bishop Stortford's famous golf club.

When it comes to dancing, she is an enthusiastic amateur.

'Pop me in a nightclub or on the dance floor and I'll just throw myself round and love it,' she says. 'For enthusiasm I get ten out of ten.'

The London-born broadcaster reveals she had two dance lessons before her wedding to James Haggar 12 years ago, but things didn't quite go to plan on the big day.

'James doesn't embrace dancing, so I wanted us to look like we weren't completely out of sync when we did our first dance,' she recalls. 'But we went a bit too far the other way. The routine we learnt was a little bit too choreographed and a little bit too much for us to take on, I think, on our wedding day. When it came to the bit where we could let loose and not be formal, I went a bit mad and went flying in the air in a puff of wedding dress, landed on my butt and James gallantly came over and picked me up!'

Naga studied journalism before landing a job as a City reporter on the *Evening Standard*. She moved into TV, reporting for Reuters Financial Television, CNBC Europe and Channel 4, before becoming a regular presenter on BBC *Breakfast* in 2009. When Strictly beckoned, however, she couldn't wait to get on her feet.

'If anyone offers you the chance to be taught to dance by a professional, you'd be mad to say no,' she says. 'As scary as it is, and it is a really scary prospect, I'm someone who loves learning new things and trying to be the best I can, so this is an opportunity to live life and enjoy it. It would have been churlish to say no.'

Before slipping on her dancing shoes, the 41-year-old got some tips from her colleague and former Strictly contestant, Carol Kirkwood.

'Carol told me to just enjoy it and don't worry what anybody thinks about you as a dancer because we are not dancers, we are trying to learn to dance. It's not going to be a judgement on you as a person but a judgement on your dancing. You're being given the best opportunity to learn so just enjoy it.'

As a dance novice, Naga admits to a touch of the jitters.

'I'm going to be out of my comfort zone, which no one looks forward to,' she says. 'But whatever happens I'll look back on it and go "Wow, what an experience."'

Pasha
Kovalev

Former champ Pasha Kovalev has been in the final for three out of his five years on the show, and finally landed the Strictly crown with series 12 partner Caroline Flack.

Last year, he danced up a storm with BBC weathergirl Carol Kirkwood and this year he is waltzing her Breakfast colleague, Naga Munchetty, off the sofa.

'Naga has only had a couple of dance lessons in her life so we are pretty much starting from scratch,' he says. 'But she has good rhythm and she's determined. We're building and building, bit by bit.

'She is used to working under pressure and is very competitive. She is nervous about dancing live but she is determined not to let that affect her performance.'

The BBC presenter may not know how to dance yet but she's used to winning trophies on the golf course, and Pasha thinks that could help her get in the swing.

'Naga is a really hard worker and is really putting a lot into training,' he says. 'She is extremely fit, because she plays so much golf, and she has core strength which really helps in dancing.'

While she welcomed the Latin, however, Pasha's new pupil was not quite sure about the more formal dances.

'Naga was very nervous of the ballroom at first because she didn't think she'd be any good,' he says. 'But she is picking it up really well and is loving it now. The golf doesn't really help with that because the ballroom hold is a very unnatural position to be in for any length of time so, no matter what your usual sport is, it can be uncomfortable.'

The Russian pro took up dancing at eight and, at 21, he moved to the US with his dancing partner Anya Garnis, where they reached the finals of the US Open four years running. In 2007, Pasha joined *So You Think You Can Dance?* and, four years later, moved the UK to compete on *Strictly Come Dancing*. In his first two years he reached the final, with Chelsee Healey and Kimberley Walsh, before taking the title in two years later with Caroline Walsh. He was the first pro to make the final three times and still holds the record for the highest number of 10s, with 61.

Although he and Carol left in week 7 in series 13, Pasha says it was sunshine all the way.

'Last year was fantastic,' he says. 'Carol was wonderful to work with. She was really hard-working and enthusiastic and really enjoyed herself.

'The training was intense and she was up at 3am every morning for work but she never lost her beautiful smile!'

Around the WORLD

Since Strictly first hit UK screens in 2004, the format has gone global and has sold to over 50 countries. Known as Dancing with the Stars in the US and Australia and by many other names across the world, the show has been seen across six of the seven continents.

Over 2,500 episodes and 270 series have been recorded to date, and every week of last year a local version of *Dancing with the Stars* was in production somewhere across the globe.

In 2014, Costa Rica, Serbia, Romania and Slovenia joined the global family.

Kim Kardashian, David Hasselhoff, Pamela Anderson and even astronaut Buzz Aldrin have competed in the US version of Dancing with the Stars. President Obama once delayed an important speech on Libya to avoid clashing with the show.

Slovenia, birthplace of former champ Aljaž Skorjanec, was the 50th country to adopt the show.

Former champ Darren Bennett has judged the show in **Lebanon**.

In **Italy**, a member of royalty, Prince Emanuele Filiberto of Savoy, won series 5 of Ballando con le Stelle.

In **Finland** the show's name translates to Tanssii Tähtien Kanssa and in Poland it's Taniec z Gwiazdami.

In Georgia, the show is filmed in a circus tent as there isn't a suitable studio available.

The latest country to launch its own version is the **Philippines**, in 2016.

Bollywood star Madhuri Dixit has judged two series of the Indian version of the show, Jhalak Dikhhla Jaa.

International football star David Ginola scored third place in France's Danse avec les stars in 2011.

In 2004, the year Strictly kicked off, Australia was keen to join the party. It was the first country to adopt the format and screened as Dancing with the Stars in the same year. Neighbours actress Kimberley Davies and model Vogue Williams are among the celebrities who have competed.

Craig Revel Horwood judged three series in New Zealand and Brendan Cole judged five.

Ore Oduba

It's been an exciting year for Ore Oduba. The sports presenter spent most of the summer in Rio, following Team GB's triumphs at the Olympic Games, before stepping straight into his brand-new dance shoes to take on the Strictly challenge.

'I'm having the best time!' says the BBC *Breakfast* star. 'I can't think of a better end to the year than this. I got married last year – that was a very good end of year – but this is right up there.

'I've been really lucky because when I was growing up I wanted to be a sportsperson, but that failed, so I always wanted to be around sportspeople and the Olympics was the pinnacle. To be there and on the front line was just amazing. Then to step off the plane, and almost literally, straight on to the dance floor of *Strictly Come Dancing* is mind-blowing.'

The 29-year-old studied sports science at Loughborough University before joining *Newsround* in 2008 and switching to the *Breakfast* team and *BBC 5 Live* in 2014. But he's not the only one from the BBC sofa to be trying out his dancing skills in this series – he'll be up against colleague Naga Munchetty.

'We've been working together day after day, and she kept that little secret all to herself. But it was comforting to know I would be doing it with a mate because it is going to be such an incredible experience and everything is better shared.

'What will be really interesting is after the first dance, when we're both back on the BBC sofa going, "Are you all right? How's the recovery?"'

Ore admits the first week of training in the height of summer was tough but says he loved every minute.

'It's been the best,' he reveals. 'It was record temperatures and I have never sweated so much in my life. The clothes I wore are in the bin! It was intense but it was the best way to start learning, by throwing yourself into it.'

While he loves the training, Ore says the real challenge could be facing the fearsome foursome at the end of the dance.

'There will be times when it's hard but you have to take the criticism as part of the whole experience. The judges' views are part of the show and it helps people at home to understand more about the dance, but it's also what we the contestants can learn from.

'I am out to impress all the judges. It'll be an honour to dance in Len's final series; he's been The Godfather for so many years. But if I can get Bruno up on his feet, maybe even on the table ... I'll be very happy!'

Joanne Clifton

Grimsby girl Joanne returns this series to join brother Kevin and sister-in-law Karen in the bid for the glitter ball. But who does she think will get furthest in the competition?

'Hopefully not Kevin!' she jokes. 'I'm going to do everything I can to stop that happening. I'd love Karen to be there, with Will Young, but not Kevin. I won't hear the end of it!'

Joanne, whose parents are former World Champions Keith and Judy Clifton, grew up dancing with her big brother and later specialised in ballroom, moving to Bologna to train at 14 before becoming World Ballroom Showdance Champion in 2013. But while Kevin reached the series final for the third time, last series Joanne didn't let her own triumphs go unnoticed.

'I won the Christmas special with Harry Judd,' she laughs. 'So I do like to tell him that the only glitter ball in the family is mine and that it's in Grimsby on my mother's mantelpiece.'

For series 14, Joanne is getting BBC *Breakfast* presenter Ore Oduba off his couch and into his dancing shoes. As far as his rehearsals are going, it's 'sofa' so good.

'Ore's very talented,' she says. 'I think he'll be great at the Latin because he moves well and his body is very flexible and rhythmic. Ballroom-wise, I'm finding it hard to keep his body still, in the frame, because he wants to move around. As soon as he nails that he'll be great because when he gets his arms into a good position he looks perfect.

'He got the routine the first day but then he had a few mind blanks – everything went in and then we went back over it and he'd lost it a bit, but it came back.'

The only problem the former World Champion has now is getting her eager new pupil to take a rest stop.

'He's brilliant. He wants to work,' says Joanne. 'He keeps saying he doesn't want breaks and doesn't even want lunch. I tell him he has to eat because we're practising for seven hours straight so he needs the energy. But it's great that he just wants to keep going because that's how I used to train when I was competing, so he has the mentality of a competitor.

'Ore has said he's always dreamt of being trained like a top athlete and, in the first week, he just stopped in rehearsal, when I was working him really hard and said "I'm living out a dream here." It was actually quite emotional.'

It's not all work and no play, though. 'He's keeps calling me Mr Miyagi, from *The Karate Kid*, because I get him to repeat everything over and over again so he says it's like the famous "wax on, wax off" scene. So we're training hard but we do have a lot of fun.'

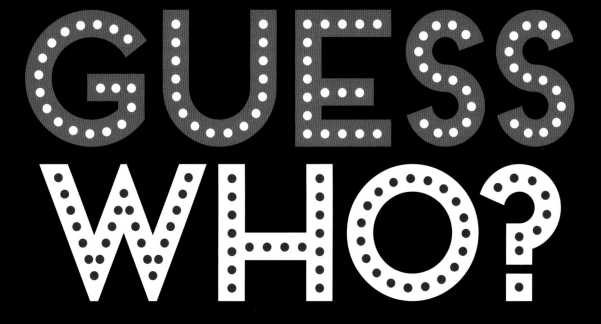

GUESS WHO?

Whether it's Len's cry of 'I'll pickle my walnuts' or Craig's 'dis-ah-ster darling', the wit and wisdom of the four judges has us chortling into our cuppa every Saturday night. But can you identify the celebs (and a pro) from these ballroom gems?

1. 'It was like a cow pat on Countryfile. Hot and steamy.' Len on a dramatic tango in series 13.

2. 'You flew across the floor like a rampant crab.' Len thinks one of the pro's American smooth moves is a bit fishy.

3. 'It was like watching a stork who'd been struck by lightning.' Whose series 13 jive had Craig in a flap?

4. 'You did a tango like ET's mum.' Bruno sends his message home to one series 8 legend.

5. 'There you were like two sizzling sausages on a BBQ… Your bum was bionic.' Len gets hot and bothered over a series 13 salsa.

6. 'You were wriggling around like a slug in salt.' Craig's earthy comment on a series 11 salsa.

7. 'You brought tears to my eyes.' Darcey gets emotional over a series 13 rumba.

8. 'You look like the queen of the night. But you dance like the Walking Dead.' A Halloween horror that saw a celeb emerge from a coffin which gave Bruno the chills.

9. 'It was Benny Hill's version of the paso but everything was there.' Bruno's comic turn on a series 9 contestant.

10. 'You have a hip action that could crack coconuts.' Which series 12 actor sent Craig nuts for his salsa?

11. 'You're the new age Carmen Miranda.' Darcey's fruity take on a singer's sizzling samba in series 12.

12. 'You floated across that dance floor like butter on a hot crumpet.' Len's mouth was watering after a floaty foxtrot in series 12.

1. Anita Rani 2. Gleb Savchenko 3. Jeremy Vine 4. Ann Widdecombe 5. Kellie Bright 6. Rachel Riley 7. Jay McGuiness 8. Nancy Dell'Olio 9. Russell Grant 10. Jake Wood 11. Pixie Lott 12. Frankie Bridge

WORDSearch

Are you eagle-eyed as well as fleet of foot? Waltz around our
word search and see how many you can spot.

T	H	J	K	F	N	S	H	L	F	J	N	F	A	G
P	A	S	O	D	O	B	L	E	G	I	A	F	B	N
G	X	M	Z	T	L	A	G	I	Y	H	U	E	M	V
N	E	T	E	N	P	G	V	N	C	Y	H	B	J	A
Y	T	N	Q	R	M	W	D	A	N	C	E	O	F	F
R	H	I	D	P	I	R	H	B	W	F	H	R	V	O
E	G	T	G	P	H	C	M	X	U	N	R	I	N	X
B	I	A	S	C	R	Y	A	B	A	D	Y	U	F	T
Z	T	L	A	W	E	S	E	N	N	E	I	V	S	R
S	L	S	C	A	V	U	G	E	S	J	R	N	O	O
P	L	E	B	A	L	L	R	O	O	M	O	P	G	T
A	A	M	A	Z	B	R	O	O	M	H	O	I	N	C
J	U	I	H	A	W	M	V	A	G	L	K	O	A	G
R	U	H	F	J	D	Q	A	E	K	Q	A	R	T	K
H	D	C	E	V	I	J	E	S	T	Z	H	N	G	H

American smooth   Dance off   Latin   Samba
Ballroom   Foxtrot   Paso doble   Tango
Cha-cha   Jive   Rumba   Viennese waltz

STRICTLY Quiz

Are you a Strictly superfan? Quickstep through our quiz and see if it's a 'ten from Len' or a 'dance disaster'.

1 Which dance was added in series 7 and is still danced in the main show?

2 Name the three actors who have been crowned Strictly champions?

3 Kevin had never been in the dance-off before series 13. But how many times was he left battling it out in the ballroom last year?

4 Who is the only professional to have won the main series trophy twice?

5 Which two professionals have been on the show the longest?

6 Which professional has danced in the most finals?

7 How long is the average Strictly routine?

8 What song did Louis Smith and Flavia Cacace choose for their winning show dance in series 10?

9 Which American superstar guest judged in series 12?

10 Who was the first celebrity partner for Aljaž Skorjanec?

11 Which couple scored two perfect 40s in the final of the last series?

12 Which two judges have also sat on the panel of the US show *Dancing with the Stars*?

13 Which celebrity was fired from a cannon at Wembley in 2011?

Answers 1. Charleston 2. Jill Halfpenny, Tom Chambers and Kara Tointon 3. Twice 4. Aliona Vilani – with Harry Judd in 2011 and Jay McGuiness in 2015 5. Brendan Cole and Anton du Beke 6. Pasha Kovalev 7. 90 seconds 8. Take That, 'Rule the World' 9. Donny Osmond 10. Abbey Clancy 11. Kellie Bright and Kevin Clifton 12. Len Goodman and Bruno Tonioli 13. Russell Grant

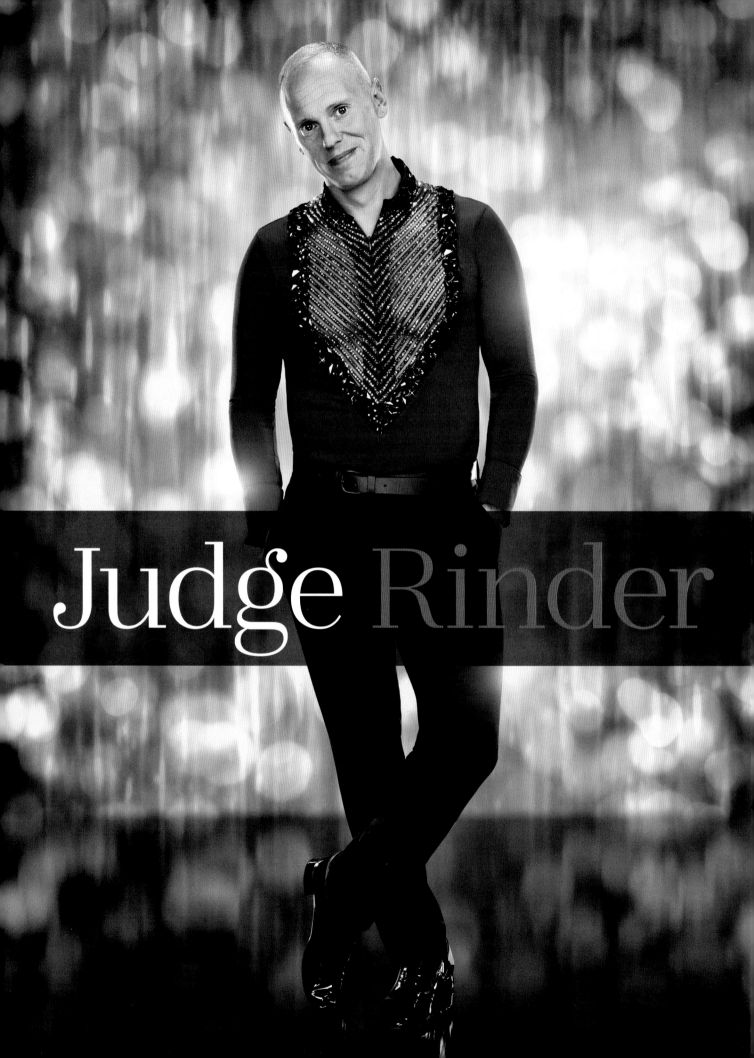

Judge Rinder

Barrister Judge Rinder will be giving Craig Revel Horwood a run for his money if he disagrees with the comments from the bench. But the legal eagle — known for his arch comments on his courtroom show Judge Rinder — is relishing the idea of sparring with Strictly's strictest critic.

'Craig is not really allowed to shout and tell people they are silly, like I do,' he laughs. 'He has to find more creative language, like a benevolent headmistress. Even when he thinks someone is terrible he has to find something to say to suggest they can improve. Thankfully I never have to do that.'

Judge Rinder grew up in London and studied at Manchester University before embarking on his legal career. He was called to the bar in 2001, specialising in international fraud, and has been involved in many high-profile prosecutions. In 2014, he began presiding over his TV court in the popular show bearing his name.

Despite his caustic reputation, Judge Rinder has a heart-warming reason for his decision to join Strictly. 'The main reason is as my grandparents get older it's a show they absolutely love. My grandma is not very

well and this is probably the last chance I will get to appear on the show and her to watch it. Although they've always been unconditionally proud of me I think there is something magical about being able to take part in something that gives them such joy and escapism.

'Also, I wanted to learn a new skill and I love the programme. It's one of the few programmes that, whatever your age or background, people are excited to share in. It's totally levelling and I love that. Plus it will be fun for someone to judge me, I suppose.'

The 38-year-old is at the peak of physical fitness, working out regularly in the gym and running long distances, and he says he is in it to win it.

'I didn't realise how competitive I was,' he reveals. 'I do marathons so I'm competitive against myself rather than anybody else. It's not that I'm indifferent to other people. Other people are splendid some of the time and everybody here is lovely. But against myself I am very competitive and I want to do better each week, definitely.'

He's also set his sights firmly on the final. 'For some reason people get subscripted into the programme and say, "I just want to get to Blackpool",' he says. 'Rubbish! I want to win.'

Oksana
Platero

Judge Rinder couldn't believe his luck when he was partnered with Oksana – because he'd been learning Russian especially for the show.

The Strictly newcomer, who is actually from Ukraine, is only one of two Russian-speaking female professionals – and she seemed impressed with the legal eagle's linguistic skills.

'He can say a couple of words,' she reveals. 'He hasn't spoken to me much in Russian but whatever he said was good.

'I must say his dancing is a lot better than his Russian at the moment. It's better that way because right now dancing is more important!'

Oksana started dancing at the age of six, and her many awards include Ukraine National Youth champion, National US Champion and USDC World Professional Rising Star Champion. At 18, she moved to the US where she danced as part of the professional troupe on *Dancing with the Stars* for five seasons, but she says *Strictly Come Dancing* is a dream come true.

'I was extremely happy because it's the job that every dancer dreams of,' she reveals. 'I was waiting for a while to find out if I had been chosen and that waiting period felt like for ever but, as soon as I heard, I started packing my bags, a month before I had to leave. Then I packed way too much stuff! But it's been a very pleasant experience and I am so happy to be here and part of such a wonderful production.

'On *Dancing with the Stars* in the US, I didn't have a celebrity partner, but I danced in all the professional performances, so it's extremely exciting for me to be in a position where I have a partner and I can test myself as a teacher and see how far I can push him and push myself. Judge Rinder is definitely the right pupil for me to do that with.'

It seems the new recruit has already tamed the truculent judge.

'I know his sharp tongue is what he is known for because that's what he does for a living, telling people what's wrong and what's right and being very strict. But now the tables are turned and he's the one that has to listen and he's doing great. He is taking my directions and showing a lot of respect.

'I'm sure he'll be more feisty with the judges than with me because he has absolute respect for everything I say, which I love. But everybody is looking forward to seeing how he talks back to the judges and so am I. They will be hilarious.'

'He really surprised me – in a good way. I would say his weakness is that he likes to talk a lot. He concentrates and is really trying his best. He has an amazing attitude!'

From PAGE to SCREEN

Creating the perfect look for each dance is crucial. Before reaching for her brushes, hair and make-up designer Lisa Armstrong puts pen to paper to sketch her ideas and chart her colour scheme.

Here she talks us through a striking design for Georgia May Foote's paso doble. 'Because it's such a dramatic dance you can be much more fierce with the make-up,' she explains. 'Normally you would never do strong eyes with strong lips but with the paso the rule book is thrown out.

'Always start with the eyes, because you don't want eyeshadow or glitter dropping on to the made-up skin below. Begin with clean, make-up-free moisturised skin.'

Eyes

1. Prep the eye area with an eye base or concealer.
2. With a black eyeshadow, draw the outline of the eye shape from the inner corner, along the socket line to the outer

Georgia May Foote's dramatic make-up matched the drama of the paso doble.

corner, lifting the flick to the edge of the eye area and then back down to the outer corner. This creates a dramatic winged effect.

3. Black is quite harsh, so to soften it use a navy-blue shadow on the lids and blend into the black, making sure the edges are blended.

4. Use a black eyeliner through the lash line and follow the curve of the eye at the end. Never bring the flick downwards. You want to elongate the eye so bring it outwards and up.

5. Use a matt peach powder to blend into the edges of the black and blue, to soften the 'mask' effect.

6. Add thick fluffy lashes that wing out at the outer corner.

7. Bring the eyeliner into the inner corner of the eye to create a point then underneath to create a line up to the flick so that everything is joined.

8. Draw black eyeliner along the lower inner rim of your eyelid.

9. Accentuate the eyebrows, filling in gaps for a strong look. Using a make-up brush, start at the inner corner of the brow, move it into the middle, above the pupil, where it should be thick and then to the outer corner where it should taper out. Fill that eyebrow in with a soft pencil to suit your own hair colour and skin tone. Or use a light brown powder shadow to get a softer effect.

10. Clean the whole face with wipes or cleanser and use a Q-tip to perfect the line from the inner eye, underneath, and up to the end, blending the point of the flick out at the end for a winged effect.

TOP TIP

To create that fierce line, take a tiny bit of surgical tape and stick it on the outer corner of your eye at the angle you want, going upwards towards the hairline. Draw along the edge then bring it backwards down through the socket line. Take away the tape and fill in with your blue and black eyeshadow, then blend.

Cheeks

1. Moisturise and add under-eye concealer.

2. Now apply foundation. We use a buffer brush to get a really even skin tone. This stimulates the blood cells so the skin's own luminosity shines through.

3. Use a light-reflecting powder under the eyes – essential when under the Strictly spotlight!

4. Take a contouring palette and, using a darker tone and a fine brush, lightly sweep underneath your cheekbone, browbone and jawbone to add definition.

5. Add the lighter tone to the cheeks to give them a dewy glow.

6. With a blusher brush, apply a peachy colour to the apple of the cheeks and blend in.

Lips

1. For this look we use a two-tone lip – known as the ombre lip – which really stands out on the dance floor.

2. Use a liner that is a tone darker than the lipstick and then fill in with the red, blending out harsh lines.

Now for the sparkle

1. Powder your face in the T-zone area, across the forehead, down the nose and chin.

2. Place a piece of paper towel under the eye.

3. Dip a brush into a mixing medium or petroleum jelly (essential to make the glitter stick) then dip into a pot of black

glitter and shake off the excess, to avoid droppage.

4. Press into the eyelid and move it all along the lash line, so you've covered your whole eyelid. Leave to set for a few seconds.

5. Set with a make-up setting spray.

TOP TIP

★ When you move your eyes or turn your face, glitter adds a real wow factor.

★ You can buy glitter pens that are cheap, come in all colours and are really good. Don't use a gel glitter because that moves and makes a mess.

★ If you're feeling brave use a nice fine loose make-up glitter. If not, go with glitter pens.

Styling the hair

On Strictly Saturday the dancers are in and out of the hair department all day, being crimped, curled and clipped up. Stylist Lisa Davy works closely with Lisa Armstrong to create the perfect hairstyle for each dance. 'The dancers get their hair done quite early in the day so it has to be reset throughout. They often wear rollers throughout rehearsals and band call, but it needs to be totally ready for the dress run in the afternoon and often redone for the show. 'We are fixing things all the time because they are sweating a lot and being thrown around a lot. As the day goes on and more and more product is added, it often becomes rock hard and doesn't move.'

Get the look

For Georgia's paso doble look, Lisa and her team pulled her hair back to make a Mohawk on top, to expose the drama on her face, but with flowing tresses down her back.

Here is Lisa's step-by-step guide:

1. Section off the hair and pull back the sides tightly, so you are left with the centre panel of hair.

2. Secure the side sections with bands and plenty of clips.

3. Backcomb the top section and add texturing powder then use crimping irons or a conical wand on the roots to add texture and volume.

4. Shape each piece of hair to build up the shape of the Mohawk and secure with pins.

5. Add hair extensions (optional) to get the length at the back.

6. Spray generously with hairspray.

7. Add braids and ribbons for extra detail. We used pieces of fabric to match the deep-blue dress.

Tameka
Empson

Soap star Tameka is thrilled to be joining the Strictly bubble and can't wait to show off her moves.

The *EastEnders* star gave up her childhood lessons of ballet and tap when she went to stage school, but says she has always had an interest in dance.

'I'm slightly delirious but I cannot put into words how much I am enjoying this thing,' she says. 'I have always wanted to do Strictly. I love to dance and I think the scheduling of the show is great because it's the autumn and winter, it's not nice outside and to put on the TV and watch something so glamorous is perfect. I have always thought "I'd like to be a part of that one day."'

The London-born actress, who plays Kim Fox in *EastEnders*, has more than the dances to keep her on her toes. She's juggling rehearsal time with a full filming schedule and being a mum to her two-year-old daughter.

'How am I doing it? I don't know,' she laughs. 'Bit by bit! Kellie Bright did the same last year and I was saying "How are you doing this?"

'But I enjoy everything I do and I am loving *EastEnders*, loving Strictly and loving being mum to my daughter, even though, being in the terrible twos, she can give me a bit of lip from time to time. It's all fun so I'm not seeing it as work. I do a lot of prepping, so I sort my little girl's clothes for the week and work out dinner plans in advance and then hope it all falls into place.

'But there's a lot of coffee going on. Mocha is my best friend.'

Another new friend is Gorka Marquez, the Strictly pro currently putting her through her paces.

'Gorka is a lovely guy,' she reveals. 'I call him Gorka the corker. I feel as if I've known him for such a long time already. He's easy to talk to, very experienced and he really knows his stuff. He doesn't only tell me the steps but he tells me the history of the steps and why the dance is the way it is. He's a great teacher.'

The 39-year-old star is physically fit, although she admits, 'I like to say I go to the gym, but I say it more than I do it!'

But don't be fooled by her bubbly sense of humour. Tameka is in it to win it.

'I'm taking it very seriously,' she says. 'When I go out there I can't hide behind a character. It's not Kim doing it, it's myself, so I want to make sure I do it to the best of my ability and I don't let myself or Gorka down. I want to hold that glitter ball!'

She also promises to have a good time along the way.

'I don't go out often so this is my going out,' she says. 'You won't find a bigger fan of the costumes, sparkles and bling. I go in as a blank canvas and I say, "do what you will". It's just great. I love to be pampered and they pamper me, so all I have to do is give a good routine.

'I only wish I had my week 13 figure on week 1!'

Gorka
Marquez

Strictly newcomer Gorka got a warm welcome from his fellow professionals before he'd even set foot in the country. The Spanish dancer, who moved to London from New York, was overwhelmed by the messages he received from his new colleagues.

'They were amazing,' he explains. 'All of them were friendly and nice to me. Even before I came they were messaging me saying, "Whatever you need, if you need a place to stay, tell me." They helped me with everything and made me feel like part of the family, so it was easy to fit in with them when I arrived.'

Gorka was a relative latecomer to dance, taking it up at the grand old age of 12, but in 2010 he represented Spain in the World Latin Championships and two years later he reached the semi-finals of the WDSF World Cup. After turning professional, Gorka toured Africa and China in the stage show Burn the Floor before settling in New York. But he always had his sights set on Strictly.

'It's a dream come true,' he says. 'As a ballroom dancer, one of the greatest things you can do in your life is to join *Dancing with the Stars* or *Strictly Come Dancing* but to go straight on the biggest show in the UK … wow! So I am up in the clouds a little bit.'

For his first series, Gorka has been coupled with *EastEnders* actress Tameka Empson – and it sounds like they're having a ball.

'Tameka is an amazing lady, both as a person and as a student,' he reveals. 'I'm so happy and I think everyone will fall in love with her. In rehearsals, she is super-energetic and super-efficient, everything is going well. She's so funny and has such a personality, she makes me laugh all the time so it's great.'

But all that fun isn't getting in the way of some hard work in the rehearsal studio. 'She is very focused on the job and working really hard. They are long days for her because she has to start filming on *EastEnders* very early and then she has five hours of rehearsals but, even if I say "Let's have a five-minute break", she says "No, let's do it one more time." She's very determined.'

When he's not in the training sessions, Gorka is getting to know his new home, with the help of his Scottish fiancée, musical theatre dancer Lauren Sherida.

'I didn't have too much time to see a lot of London before we started training but the area where I live is very nice and I love it,' he says. 'I love big cities because there are a lot of things to do, lots of places to go and everything is open so I think I'll be very happy here.'

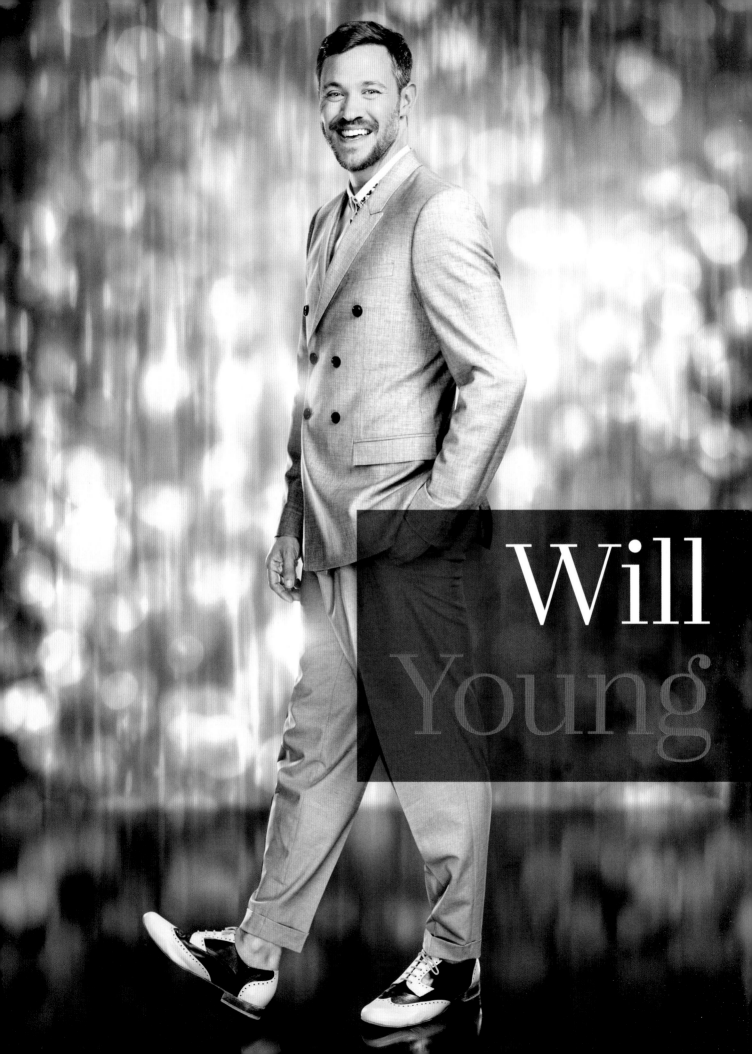

Will
Young

After 15 years in the charts, singer Will Young clearly has a musical ear, but it is the acting side of the routines he is most looking forward to.

'I love dressing up as different characters in my music videos,' says Will. 'With Strictly, every dance will bring a different character depending on the style and the song. That's part of the fun.'

Chart-topper Will was born in Berkshire and shot to fame on *Pop Idol* in 2001, when he beat Gareth Gates to become the first-ever winner of the worldwide franchise. Despite the historic success, and a string of top ten hits, Will says winning is not his motivation for taking to the dance floor.

'I won't get competitive,' he insists. 'I already did a talent show 15 years ago, and I wasn't even competitive on that. What I love about *Strictly* is that it's about the experience.

'I do know some former contestants and all I've ever heard is that it's just the most incredible experience. It's a family show, but what I love most is seeing people grow. The dancing I have done in my music career has built my confidence no end. Initially I couldn't even stand onstage without holding my microphone stand and it took me five years to do that so I just love seeing people grow in confidence and *Strictly* does that.'

Appearing on the show last year, as a guest performer, clinched his passion for the show.

'I genuinely am borderline obsessive,' he jokes. 'I have wanted to do it for a while and it's never tied in with the music and the acting. I performed on the show last year and I just loved it. I love the vibe. It felt like a real family and I said to my manager at the time, "If they ask I'll do it."'

Having faced the *Pop Idol* panel, at the tender age of 22, Will is prepared to take on the judges – even Craig.

'He's a softie, deep down,' says the 37-year-old star. 'The judges give really good critiques and when I've watched the show, the contestants take that on board so those things can only be positive.'

But he's in no doubt as to his favourite judge.

'Len! I love him,' he laughs.

Let's hope Mr Goodman doesn't tell Will to 'Leave Right Now' after his first foray onto the dance floor.

Karen Clifton

After being paired with singer Will Young on this year's launch show, Karen instantly tested his strength and ability in hold – by leaping into his arms with sheer joy.

'I was quite happy,' she laughs. 'I'm still holding on!

'I was the last pro to be paired and it was lovely to be paired up with Will because I know that he will throw himself into it, and that's what I really like about my previous celebrities. They embraced Strictly and have absolutely loved dancing.

'In the first group dance, Will looked like he was having a complete blast. That's what I love – the happiness and joy that he has for the dance really comes through.'

With a pop career spanning 15 years behind him, Will is used to dancing in music videos but Karen insists that's not necessarily an advantage.

'The discipline behind it is there but nothing compares to partner dancing,' she explains. 'It's different when you are dancing on your own. In fact, a lot of the other celebs have had some form of training but it's a whole different world when it comes to what we do.'

Even so the bubbly dancer – who wed Kevin Clifton in 2015 – believes she can turn this pop idol into a ballroom king.

'He has an amazing frame,' she explains. 'He does slouch a little bit at times but I think, with some practice, he might be more of a ballroom guy. Then again, once that party music starts he might want to start shaking those hips around and go Latin crazy on me. My guess is that he'll be the Gene Kelly of this year.'

Venezuelan-born Karen, who starred in *So You Think You Can Dance?* in the US before joining Strictly in series 10, was paired with Jeremy Vine last year and she says they had a ball.

'To me Jeremy was an absolute star and he really inspired me,' she says. 'I came in this year feeling really confident and that's partly down to Jeremy. He taught me that it doesn't matter how much of a novice you are, as long as you try hard and you do it because you love it, that's all that matters.'

After being eliminated in week 8, however, Karen has one major ambition for the new series.

'I just want to make it to Blackpool!' she says. 'I made it with Mark Wright, but my first year with Nicky Byrne, we did Wembley instead, and last year, I was out too early, so I am definitely hoping to make it to Blackpool. And, of course, I would like to get to dance all the dances with Will!'

Neil Jones

Although he's new to the official Strictly line-up, Neil has been part of the team for the last three years, helping out with the choreography and stepping in when an extra dancer was needed.

'I grew up with the original *Come Dancing* so when *Strictly* started I was hooked from the beginning,' he reveals. 'To be asked to come on as a professional is a massive honour.'

The British dancer is married to fellow pro and dance partner Katya Jones. The pair are three-time winners of the World Amateur Latin Championships and, in 2015, they were crowned World Professional Latin Show Dance Champions. Appropriately, the couple met at the Strictly mecca of Blackpool.

'It was the British Open and Katya came without a dancing partner, to watch,' he recalls. 'I was competing with another partner but I ended the partnership the next day and then we had a try-out. Two weeks later we started dancing together.'

Romance blossomed and the couple tied the knot three years ago. But Neil, who was born on a British Army Camp in Germany, admits he is still not fluent in his Russian bride's mother tongue.

'I understand a little bit,' he says. 'I had an Ukrainian partner before and I chose to learn a few words so I would know when she was saying bad things about me. When I met Katya I told her, "Just so you're aware, I do know a little bit of Russian!"'

Although Neil won't be paired with a celebrity this year, he'll be dancing, choreographing and commentating on *It Takes Two*. But he could also stand in as a double for Greg Rutherford.

'Everybody thinks that Greg and I look alike, especially from behind,' laughs Neil. 'We're getting it constantly, both of us. But I hope his dancing is better than my long jump. He's already given us all a challenge to see how far we could jump from a standing position. Aljaž won but I wasn't great!'

Having turned 21 just the day after her first rehearsals, Chloe Hewitt is Strictly's youngest-ever professional dancer. But she has plenty of experience, having started dancing at seven and competing with dance partner AJ Pritchard at 11.

'As a kid, I went along to AJ's parents' dance school and it started as a Saturday morning social class,' she reveals. 'Then his parents said their son wanted to start competing and would I be interested in being his partner in competitions, so I said "yes".'

The talented pair went on to set records by becoming the National Youth Latin Champions for three years in a row from 2012–2014. Last year they became British Open Youth Latin Champions and European Youth Latin Champions.

'We've been partners for 10 years, which is quite unusual because in the dance world partners swap and change like nobody's business, but AJ and I have stuck it out and it's always worked. We've never really argued, which has helped.'

Having grown up watching the show, the Chester lass is happy to put the competing on hold while she takes to the Strictly floor.

'I was eight years old when the show started and I've watched every series, so appearing on this show is huge for me. It feels so surreal.'

Although Chloe won't be partnered with a celebrity during this series she will be kept busy with group dances, guest-star musical numbers and providing commentary on It Takes Two. And she'll be cheering on AJ and his partner Claudia Fragapane.

'I can't wait to see him dance with Claudia because I have high expectations of her,' she says. 'I think she'll be a force to reckon with.'

1 2 3 4 5 6 7 8 9 10

BBC Books, an imprint of Ebury Publishing
20 Vauxhall Bridge Road, London SW1V 2SA

BBC Books is part of the Penguin Random House group
of companies whose addresses can be found at
global.penguinrandomhouse.com

Penguin
Random House
UK

Text by Alison Maloney. Copyright © Woodland Books Ltd 2016
Alison Maloney has asserted her right to be identified as the
author of this Work in accordance with the Copyright, Designs and
Patents Act 1988

This book is published to accompany the television series entitled
Strictly Come Dancing first broadcast on BBC One in 2016

Executive producer: Louise Rainbow
Series producer: Sara James
Director of Entertainment, Music and Events: Roger Leatham

With thanks to Selena Harvey, Tessa Beckett, Kim Winston, Jack
Gledhill, Harriet Frost and the *Strictly Come Dancing* production team.

Strictly Come Dancing logo © BBC 2016, BBC logo © BBC 1996
Devised by the BBC and licensed by BBC Worldwide Limited
Picture credits: Celebrity, Judges and Presenter portrait shots © BBC/
Jay Brooks/Matt Burlem, Pro Dancer portrait shots © BBC/Jay Brooks/
Geraint Williams, Photos pp. 14–17, 56–59, 64–65, 78–81,
90–93 by Guy Levy © Woodland Books Ltd, photo p.38
© Mark Parker, all other images © BBC
First published by BBC Books in 2016

www.penguin.co.uk

A CIP catalogue record for this book is available from the British
Library

ISBN 9781785940903

Commissioning editor: Yvonne Jacob
Project editor: Grace Paul
Cover design: Two Associates
Designer: Clarkevanmeurs Design

Printed and bound in Italy by Rotolito Lombarda SpA

Penguin Random House is committed to a sustainable future for our
business, our readers and our planet. This book is made from Forest
Stewardship Council® certified paper.